T0129261

ISLAM

ISLAM

The Armageddon Bomb

Rev. Stephen Jumaat Abdul-Razaq

authorHOUSE®

AuthorHouse™ UK
1663 Liberty Drive
Bloomington, IN 47403 USA
www.authorhouse.co.uk
Phone: 0800.197.4150

Published by AuthorHouse 07/31/2015

ISBN: 978-1-5049-8782-0 (sc)
ISBN: 978-1-5049-8783-7 (hc)
ISBN: 978-1-5049-8781-3 (e)

Library of Congress Control Number: 2015912046

Print information available on the last page.

Dedication

To all those who have been martyred for their belief in Jehovah God and for following his only begotten son, Jesus Christ – from the apostle Stephen, who was stoned to death in the Bible days, to the twenty-eight Christians recently pulled out of their bus in Kenya and shot in the heads on the roadside and to the dozens of Coptic Christians beheaded by ISIL pouring their sacred blood into Atlantic Oceans simply for being Christians. Words can not describe the agonies suffered by Christians locked up in metal cage like rabid dogs and dipped repeatedly in the ocean until their holy and sacred lives suffocated out of them by ISIL. Even though their journey in this world was wickedly terminated by Satanists, surely they are reigning with our lord, Jesus Christ, in Christian paradise. Hallelujah.

Contents

Preface

I give glory to Almighty God, Jehovah, I AM THAT I AM, for revealing this great wisdom to man and for using me to spread this message. I have struggled with understanding the nature of Islam since I was six years old when my grandmother, who converted to Christianity although her father was a Chief Imam, gave me my first warning about Islam.

My Muslim father, Abdul Razaq, abandoned my mother while I was still in the womb, so I never set my eyes on him until I reached the age of nine. He had run away with another woman and left me at the mercy of my maternal grandmother, who was also dumped by her Muslim husband after he married younger wives.

So, while my paternal relatives tried to enrol me in Koranic school and wanted me to practise Islam, my grandmother insisted that I should follow her to church and be a good Christian. She told me that Islam is a harsh and cruel religion that shows no respect for women. This perspective is understandable, considering the way her Muslim husband and my mother's treated each of them. She also told me that Islam has no regard for the lives of people who are non-Muslim. The Koran regards them as pagans whom Muslims can kill at will, as Allah permits it.

My grandmother also urged me at such a tender age to be a Christian because men in this religion marry only one wife and love their families, but Muslims treat their multiple wives as cans of milk which they toss into a garbage bin after sucking out the contents. After hearing that, I vowed never to be a Muslim, but I was curious about them. Behold, the more I learnt about them, the more gruesome discoveries I made.

Thank God I was exposed to the danger of Islam early enough to run away from it, thus fulfilling what the Bible says in Proverbs 22: 6, "Train up a child in the way he should go: and when he is old, he will not depart from it." And as John 6: 44 states, "No man can come to me, except the Father which has sent me draw him: and I will raise him up at the last day." I thank Jesus for bringing me out of the ungodly political affiliation of Islam which I inherited by birth and for drawing me close to Jesus Christ, through his blood and divine adoption.

Growing up and seeing the intolerance, cruelty, and godless behaviour of adherents of Islam only confirmed the childhood warning from my grandmother. They take a jihadi approach to every religious issue, ready with permission from Prophet Mohammed to kill people in the most gruesome manner. They even behead their victims and place the heads on stakes for public celebration.

This readiness for combat and aggression simply removes the lies that Islam is a religion of peace and that Muslims and Christians worship the same God. Jesus Christ said in Matthew 7: 15–21:

> Beware of false prophets, which come to you in sheep's clothing, but inwardly they are ravening wolves. Ye shall know them by their fruits. Do men gather grapes of thorns, or figs of thistles? Even so every good tree brings forth good fruits; but a corrupt tree brings forth evil fruit. A good tree cannot bring forth evil fruit, neither can a corrupt tree bring forth good fruit. Every tree that brings not forth good fruit is hewn down, and cast into the fire. Wherefore by their fruits you shall know them. Not every one that said unto me, Lord, Lord, shall enter into the kingdom of heaven; but he that doeth the will of my father which is in heaven.

And in John 14: 27, he stated, "Peace I leave with you, my peace I give you; not as the world gives, give I unto you. Let not your heart be troubled, neither let it be afraid." We have seen the satanic tree of Islam and the rotten fruits it bears, indicating for sure that it is not a peaceful religion from Jehovah. Rather, Islam masquerades as an acceptable modern religion to lure unfortunate and sometimes unsuspecting followership into justifying their homicidal actions as acts of worship.

Unfortunately, for centuries, people have been too scared to openly comment on the domineering and wanton attitudes of Muslims for fear of retribution or a fatwa (death sentence) being placed on their heads such as the one author Salmon . is under. He is now living in hiding and might be for the rest of his life. Because of the fatwa on him, anyone in the Islamic religion that sees him shall bind him hand and foot, lay him on the ground like a goat, and chant, "Bisimi Laahi Rahmooni Al-Rahimi," meaning, "I start in the name of Allah ..." before slaughtering him like a goat. This type of wickedness is meant to intimidate people of other faiths or views, and it is the reason we should courageously talk about this evil ideology. Citizens of the world will be aware of the danger they live with and will know how to avoid the menace of those who follow Islam and, better still, able to handle and stop the threat they pose.

Pay rapt attention to the message in this book, and make an informed opinion about the evil child about whom our father Abraham warned us almost five thousand years ago when talking about Ishmael, the son of Hagar, and his descendants: the Ishmaelites, or the Mohammedans [Muslims and Islam]. Abraham said, "And he will be a wild man, his hand will be against every man, and every man's hand against him." (Gen. 16: 12).

Today, the Ishmaelites make up the mujahedeen (religious warriors), who follow the injunction from their hero and mentor, Prophet Mohammed. They will fight furiously and mercilessly to advance the cause of Islam, the only standing religion of the Antichrist.

And as we saw when the hijackers flew their planes into the Twin Towers on 9/11, all Muslims shall join the fight to usher in the return of Imam Mahdi, their expected messiah. They will use an Armageddon bomb to wipe off every non-Muslim from the map and install a global caliphate where all bow to Allah, the god of the sun.

This book therefore contains graphic descriptions of the potential great destruction that will hasten the end day and the return of Jesus Christ to take the elect home to himself.

The Abrahamic Religions: Judaism and Christianity

About five thousand years ago, during the formative stage of world's first God-approved religion, the world was filled with people who had no clear understanding of Jehovah, the only I Am Who I Am and the creator of heaven and earth. Rather, people's view of the universe and their immediate environment was shrouded in mystery, wonder, bemusement, amusement, amazement, ignorance, and heresy. People relied on tales with unverified information passed down from generation to generation to determine their culture, traditions, and religion. People who appeared powerful or possessed special powers were regarded as gods or idols, while objects whose candour, features, functions, or appearances seemed to be beyond human comprehension were mysterious and often idolized by the primitive people of the time too. Because various cultures of the world were in their formative stages, they chose gods and goddesses as forms of cultural identity and objects of traditional worship.

So, it was common to see people worship a god of sun simply because the sun rises and sets at a certain time of the day and because it gives them heat to dry their clothes as well as bright light to see clearly. Moon worshippers did the same because it gives them brightness at night. The same applied to stars, rocks, stones, hills, mountains, and trees, all of which people ignorantly idolized and worshipped in their lack of knowledge about the true living God, Jehovah Jireh, the creator of heaven and earth. People in the past and today also worship fellow human beings, such as warriors, champions, and celebrities.

Because Satan is the father of lies, he sees this as a great opportunity to recruit followers for himself. He possesses these gods and idols with evil supernatural power to make people fear and marvel at them, and then the people's mind-sets and total existence are based on trust and worship of these deities. Once such a god is established, goldsmiths, blacksmiths, and sculptors do everything in their power to create taboos and superstitions about their chosen idols and means of livelihood. Sadly, in conjunction with Satan, idol worshipers and craftsmen sometimes demand money, gold, silver, and animal or even human sacrifices to their gods.

In Acts 19: 35, we read of the Ephesians worshipping the goddess Diana and the image which fell down from Jupiter. In verses 37 and 38 of the same chapter, we read about some powerful clerks and sculptors of Diana dragging the apostles of Jesus Christ to court. The passage reads, "For ye have brought hitter these men, which are neither robbers of churches, nor yet blasphemers of your goddess. Wherefore if Demetrius and the craftsmen which are with him, have a matter against any man, the law is opened, and there are deputies, let them implead one another."

Earlier in the chapter, Acts 19: 24–26 confirms the evil connection between men and idols as follows:

> For a certain man named Demetrius, a silver smith, which made silver shrines for Diana, brought no small gain unto the craftsmen; Whom he called together with the workmen of like occupation, and said, Sirs, ye know that by this craft we have our wealth. Moreover you see and hear, that not alone at Ephesus, but almost throughout all Asia, this Paul hath persuaded and turned away much people, saying that there be no gods, which are made with hands; So that not only this our craft is in danger to be set at naught; but also that the temple of the great goddess Diana should be despised, and her magnificence should be destroyed, whom all Asia and the world worship.

According to Acts 14: 8–12, it was – and still is – easy for people to ignorantly turn fellow humans into gods because of a special power or strange ability they possess:

And there sat a certain man at Lystra, impotent in his feet, being a cripple from his mother's womb, who never had walked: The same heard Paul speak who steadfastly beholding him, and perceiving that he had faith to be healed, said with a loud voice, stand upright on thy feet. And he leaped and walked. And when the people saw what Paul had done, they lifted up their voices, saying in the speech of Lycaonia. The gods are come down to us in the likeness of men. And they called Barnabas, Jupiter: and Paul, Merccurius, because he was the chief speaker.

In some parts of Africa, people worship a man called Ogun Onire simply for his skills and dexterity on the battlefield and his ability and agility in winning wars for the Yoruba people, one of many Nigerian tribes. Some members of this same tribe worshipped Sango, the god of thunder, for his extraordinary power to evoke thunder and lightning to scare and burn down and defeat the enemy line. Others worshipped Yemoja, a goddess of the river. The fact is that these people are just legends with some special abilities, not God.

God created human beings for us to worship him, adore him, and have fellowship with him, and because we have derailed ourselves from this purpose by following other gods, Jehovah always find ways to bring man back to himself and away from the fangs of the great snake, Satan.

In Genesis 12: 1–5, the Bible says:

> Now the Lord had said unto Abram. Get thee out of thy country, and from thy kindred, and from thy father's house, unto a land that I will show thee: And I will make of thee a great nation,

> And I will bless thee, and make thy name great; and thou shalt be a blessing; and I will bless them that bless thee, and curse him that curses thee; and in thee shall all families of the earth be blessed. So Abram departed as the Lord had spoken unto him; and Lot went with him: and Abram was seventy and five years old when he departed Haran. And Abram took Sarai his wife, and Lot his brother's son and all their substance that they had gathered, and souls that they had gotten in Haran; and they went forth to go into the land of Canaan they came.

As we learn later in scripture, God's purpose for Abraham was to create a new name, a new country, and a new people to set him apart from his pagan background and homeland. He took Abraham and his family into the land of Canaan, where people would worship Jehovah only, free from idols and bloodshed. Jehovah planned to make them his special people on earth, from which Jesus Christ, the Messiah, would emerge.

Jeremiah 24: 7 reads, "And I will give them a heart to know me, I am the Lord: and they shall be my people and I will be their God: for they shall return unto me with their whole heart."

Why did God need people set apart for himself? The first experiments for reconciliation between God and humans failed, even after the great flood in the time of Noah. Due to the iniquities and the horrible sins of people, God decided to wipe them off the face of the earth. He only spared Noah and his family members, who lived according to the will of God. God instructed Noah – the only righteous man in the eyes of God – to build a ship and prepare various kinds of animals, birds, plants, and other creatures to go with him into the ark. Every other creature on open land would be wiped away by the flood; God expected the survivors to learn from history and live without sinning. Despite this sin-induced natural disaster, years down the line, humans still refused to abhor sin. However, because God vowed in Genesis 9: 11–16, using a rainbow as a reminder and swearing by his name never to destroy the earth by flood again, he decided to let people do whatever was right in their minds on earth and to reserve heaven to give the ultimate judgement for human deeds. Therefore, making a covenant with Abraham would bring to fruition God's desire for having people on earth who worshipped him.

Later in Genesis, a journey confirmed Abraham as the father of faith when he did not deny God his son Isaac, born of Sarah in their advanced age. God asked Abraham to sacrifice the lad to him as a test of his faith, as recorded in Genesis 22: 5–14. In verses 7 and 8, we read, "And Isaac spoke unto Abraham his father, and said, my father: and he said, here I am, my son. And he said, behold the fire and the wood: but where is the lamb for a burnt offering? And Abraham said, my son, God will provide Himself a lamb for a burnt offering: so they went both of them together." Verses 10–14 in the same chapter say the following:

And Abraham stretched forth his hand, and took the knife to slay his son. And the angel of the Lord called unto him out of heaven, and said, Abraham, Abraham: and he said, here I am. And he said, lay not thy hand upon the lad, neither do thou anything unto him: For now I know that thou fears God, seeing thou has not withheld thy son, thine only son from me. And Abraham lifted up his eyes, and looked, and behold behind him a ram caught in a thicket by his horns, and Abraham went and took the ram, and offered him up for a burnt offering in the stead of his son. And Abraham called the name of that place Jehovah Jireh: as it is said to this day, in the mount of the Lord it shall be seen.

Abraham called his God Jehovah Jireh (which means "God the provider"), not any other name. To Abraham, Allah was non-existent; the political slogan Allah came about four thousand years after our father Abraham, with the appearance of Mohammed.

This passage from Genesis is noteworthy. In the next chapter, we will discuss more about the Ishmaelite religion. The Muslims claimed their religion was from Abraham, whose name they translated to Ibrahim. In their version of the story of Abraham's sacrifice, told above, there is a major lie that discredits Islam as hailing from Abraham. They make the false claim that Allah asked Ibrahim to sacrifice his only son, Ishmael, to test his faith. How does this change in the narrative make sense? The aforementioned events with Abraham and Isaac happened more than three thousand years before the birth of our Lord and Saviour Jesus Christ, and Mohammed was not born until 570 years after the death of Jesus Christ. In other words, Islam cannot be older than 1,400 years old at present, as Mohammed did not start his campaign involving mass killings of Jews and other so-called pagans until he was around 40 years old. If this is the case chronologically, does it mean that another Ishmael and Ibrahim the world never knew about were created or born again to create the Ibrahim-Ishmael sacrifice story? In the age of established record-keeping, science, and advanced technology, this story would not have historian oral account recorded in the Koran dropping mysteriously from the skies of a hidden desert of Arabia. Instead, it would have happened in the full glare of modern historians; after all, many of the killings that the followers of Islam perpetrated are on record.

Let me reiterate here that Islam is not a religion that hails from Abraham, the patriarch of the Jewish and Christian religions. The only two religions that hailed from Abraham are Judaism, the religion of the Jews, and Christianity, the religion of followers of Jesus Christ, the Messiah. It is therefore a great mistake and falsehood to recognize Islam as one of the three religions of Abraham.

The Ishmaelite Religions:
Islam and Paganism

This is a volatile topic because the mullahs and ayatollahs regard themselves as the custodians of the Koran and keepers of holy Islamic shrines. To them, it is an abomination for other people (non-Muslims, or pagans) to dare comment on the faith. Penalties for such an atrocious – even blasphemous – act could range from flogging in a public square, stoning, or beheading.

In Islam, you don't ask questions. You are forced to believe, period. But the deeds of the so-called Islamic faithful and the modus operandi of the religion make us question it. One cannot help wanting to dig deep into the hearts and minds of adherents to this faith.

The world is generally told that Islam is a religion of peace and that there is no God but Allah, and Mohammed is his prophet. Many people know that Mohammed is considered the last and the greatest of God's prophets. Islam is supposedly the only religion that can take you to heaven, or Aaljannaah, and when you hear Muslims mention Prophet Isa (Jesus), the son of Mariam, Prophet Musa (Moses), and Nuruden (Noah), you could be fooled into believing that Islam and Christianity are indeed from same God and that both hailed from the patriarch Abraham. But when you see the hatred and disdain Muslims show towards Christians and other religions, especially the Jews, it will make you wonder what is happening.

I experienced a first-hand taste of Islamic cruelty when I travelled to Saudi Arabia about two decades ago. I had a Bible written in a local language, as I knew it could be dangerous to take an English Bible into the area as a migrant worker. At King Abdulaziz International Airport in Jeddah, at the immigration checkpoint, a Saudi officer saw the shape and unique design of the Bible and asked what type of book it was. I think he became suspicious and guessed what it might be, and as he held and examined it, I prayed in my spirit for Jesus Christ to reveal himself. I felt like I was in a den of lions and thought my natural life might be snuffed out within days after a possible fatwa, but I remained strong and brave and told him it was a history book in my native language. He looked at the book over and over while my heart raced, but I dare not show my panic; any confirmatory suspicion could be deadly. He spat on my Bible under the glare of every national present and threw it back into my bag and said, "Go on." I sensed relief on the faces of the colleagues travelling with me. Like Daniel in the lion's den, the God whom I served day and night had delivered me from the crescent-shaped blades of the Saudis. I later found out that possessing a Bible in Saudi Arabia is a crime of blasphemy, and attempting to convert Muslims to Christianity is punishable by the death penalty of beheading. I knew I dare not leave Saudi Arabia with the Bible. I left it with my colleagues as a testimony to the Saudis. This close brush with death made me determined to find out more about the founding of this bloodthirsty religion, as I cannot imagine how there could be peace in chopping off other people's heads and limbs.

According to the biblical account, Ishmael, the son of Abraham and Hagar, the slave woman from Egypt, was sent away from Abraham's household when his mother became arrogant and disrespectful to Sarah, her mistress. After the conception of Ishmael when Sarah remained barren, Hagar thought she could do or not do anything she wanted to in the household of Abraham, as the patriarch's inheritance would come to her son at the end of the day. But Sarah, who won the heart of her husband with her humility and respect for him (the Bible says in 1 Peter 3: 6, "Sarah obeyed her husband and called him Lord" urged Abraham to "send this slave woman and her son out of this house," and even though Abraham had a heavy heart and deep emotion for his son, God instructed him to provide for Hagar and her son and send them away, as Ishmael was not the child that God had promised Abraham; this would prevent Hagar from continuing to treat Sarah badly.

Genesis 16: 11–12 relates part of the aforementioned story as follows:

And the angel of the Lord said unto her, Behold, thou art with child, and shall bear a son, and shall call his name Ishmael; because Lord hath heard thy affliction. And he will be a wild man; his hand shall be against every man, and every man's hand against him: and he shall dwell in the presence of all his brethren.

Verse 7 describes where Hagar went. "And the angel of the Lord found her by a fountain of water in the wilderness, by the fountain in the way to Shur." This should bring to mind the desert land where Muslims now claim to be the site of the Water of Sam. According to their tradition, Ishmael cried and rubbed his heels on the ground there. He was thirsty, as they had no water for their journey, and Allah had mercy on them; a river of water gushed out of his heels, and they drank.. But how can we give credibility to Mohammed's story of the Water of Sam if he and his religion were non-existent during the time of Ishmael and Hagar?

Whether the story is genuine or not, the fact is that Ishmael is the patriarch of all Muslims, and the great nation that God promised to make him became the wild man of the wilderness. Because Ishmael was rejected by his biological father, he was forced to fall on his maternal lineage from Egypt (including part of present-day Saudi Arabia). The people of this group were idol worshippers, as evidenced in over 360 idols in Kaaba in the heart of Mecca alone, not to mention others spread around the desert of Saudi Arabia. In the lineage of Isaac, there have been Jews in existence for over 5,000 years before the birth of Jesus Christ as well as Christians after his death. However, records show that as recently as AD 610, about 1,404 years ago, the whole population of Saudi Arabia was idol worshippers until a battle Mohammed waged against them. By this time, the Roman Catholic Church was fully operational, including the office of the pope.

Therefore, common sense indicates that since the father of faith, Abraham, left Ishmael in his mother's care, the only religion Ishmael and his descendants knew was paganism, until the prophet Mohammed changed the primary religion of the area into Islam. Hence, it would be a huge miscarriage of justice and a distortion of the truth to call Islam a third religion of Abraham, even though this is what many people in the West and in the Arab world would have one believe.

There are two points to note here; we shall deal with them in more detail in subsequent chapters.

1. In the desert of Saudi Arabia, each family has its individual idols. Often, family members contend for power and honour amongst themselves, frequently resulting in inter sectorial frictions or all-out war.

2. In the Arab language, the name Allah refers to any sovereign entity; idol worshippers also referred to their objects of worship as Allah. This was evidenced in the case between Malaysian Catholic churches and the Malaysian Muslims; the latter dragged the former to court to stop them from referring to the Christian God as Allah. According to the Muslims in this case, only in Islam is God called Allah, and any non-Muslim's use of the word Allah in worship is a sacrilege punishable by death. Many Christians were beheaded or burned alive when churches were bombed in the scuffle that ensued. And then during the Christians' argument in court, they explained that for centuries before the founding of Islam, every religion in the Arab-speaking countries has referred to their deities as Allah; idol worshippers and Christians did this even before the prophet Mohammed. Therefore, the idea that Allah was a new name that God chose for himself, as Muslims claim to be true, is simply a fantasy. In other words, God did not change his name from Jehovah to Allah about 1,400 years ago. Rather, Allah is a name that that Mohammed appropriated for his newly established war machine turned into a religion to justify the killing, maiming, collective punishment, raping, and looting of innocent people as an act of worship to a sovereign God.

As mentioned previously, the Prophet Mohammed waged a battle to dominate other idol worshippers in Kaaba after carefully forming a strong army of zealot backers. Their collective aim was to eliminate rival deities and establish their own idol, Allah, as the only one worthy of Arabs' worship to obtain more followers, cash and in-kind gains, and other rewards.

Have you ever asked yourself what Jesus Christ did wrong? Despite his total obedience to the will of his father, even his death at Calvary, what made God send the so-called last and more glorious Prophet Mohammed?

Or perhaps you have wondered why Jehovah made such a drastic turn away from the teachings of humility, selflessness, loving your enemies and praying for them, turning the other cheek, eating with sinners, healing the sick, and dying for people that Jesus Christ represented. Does God now teach hanging your enemies in public squares and chasing those that failed to follow your teachings and then beheading them as a form of submission to the will of Allah, whom the prophet Mohammed represents?

Has Almighty God changed from ever-loving and merciful into ever-hateful and homicidal? The answer is an emphatic no. Jehovah says in Malachi 3: 6, "For I am the LORD, I change not; therefore ye sons of Jacob are not consumed." This is a direct condemnation of the destructive nature of Islam and the prophet Mohammed. It is also a reassurance to people descended from Abraham and Jacob that forces of human destruction are not from him. How could Jehovah change from the message of Mathew 19: 14, "But Jesus said, Suffer little children and forbid them not to come unto me, for of such is the kingdom of heaven," to the raping of children, demonstrated by the forced marriage of a nine-year-old girl to the prophet Mohammed at the age of fifty? If he tried that in Europe today, he would be jailed for child abuse and molestation. Or how can Jehovah approve the kidnapping of almost three hundred girls in their school dormitory at night in Nigeria by Boko Haram, the so-called army of Islam and adherents of the Koran? This barbaric act could only come from Satan, the father of lies.

Mohammed grabs other people's wealth after killing them, and he encourages his followers and armies (mujahideen) to do the same, as described in Koran 8. 41. "Whatever you take as spoils of war, lo! A fifth therefore is for Allah [the god of war] and for the messenger [Mohammed]." Proverbs 9: 17 states, "Stolen water and bread is sweeter." Islam gained followers as Mohammed acted like the lead pirate of the desert, killing over 3 million Jews of Arabia as well as countless other non-believers who were prosperous businesspeople. Mohammed and his followers stole the wealth and houses of these people and took their daughters and wives as prisoners of Allah. These women were then repeatedly raped, tortured, and sold as domestic slaves; this remains the culture of Arabs and Islam to this day.

Many things that take place in the Koran are barbaric; the true God, Jehovah, could never have inspired them. One such passage is as follows:

A horseman came to Mohammed and said: Apostle of Allah, I went before you and climbed a certain mountain and saw the Hawazin tribe all together with their women, cattle, and sheep gathering at Hunayn. Mohammed smiled and said: That will be the booty of the Muslims tomorrow if Allah wills.

The evil spying, lust, and robbery in broad daylight could never be from the same Jehovah who commanded in Exodus 20: 17 that thou shall not covet thy neighbour's house, thou shall not covet thy neighbour's wife, his manservant, nor his maidservant, nor his ox, nor his ass, nor anything that is thy neighbour's." How could the same God that gave this commandment for love and peace with our neighbours turn around and ask us to spy on them and ransack their possessions? No, this must be from Satan, the father of lies and hatred.

In the Koran, Mohammed promised jihadists sexual rewards on earth and in heaven. This is described in various ways in different passages. "Angels and handsome young boys as pearls well-guarded," (Koran 52. 24). "Rivers of wine" (Koran 47. 15), served with goblets filled at a gushing fountain white and delicious to those who drink it." "It will neither dull their senses nor befuddle them, (Koran 37. 40–48). "Rivers of milk of which the taste never changes; a joy to those who drink; and rivers of honey pure and clear," (Koran 47. 15). "Bosomed virgins for companion: a truly overflowing cup" (Koran 78. 31). These virgins are bashful and undefiled by man or demon.

Koran 33. 50 reads thus:

> Oh prophet: we allowed thee thy wives to whom thou has paid dowries, and the slaves whom thy right hand possess out of the booty which Allah hath granted thee, and the daughters of thy uncle, and of thy maternal aunt, who fled with thee to Medina, and any believing woman who hath given herself up to the prophet, if the prophet desired to wed her, a privilege to thee above the rest of the faithful.

This is a special benefit for the commander-in-chief of the caliphate. Who would challenge his self-appointed authority?

Now, let us examine the teaching of Jehovah about relationships with people who are related to us. In Leviticus 18: 6–13, God said:

> "None of you shall approach to any that is near of kin to him, to uncover their nakedness; I am the Lord. The nakedness of thy father, or the nakedness of thy mother, shall thou not uncover; she is thy mother; thou shall not uncover her nakedness. The nakedness of thy father's wife shall thou not uncover; it is thy father's nakedness. The nakedness of thy sister, the daughter of thy father, or daughter of thy mother, whether she be born at home, or born abroad, even their nakedness thou shall not uncover. The nakedness of thy son's daughter, or of thy daughter's daughter, even their nakedness thou shall not uncover; for theirs is thine own nakedness. The nakedness of thy father's wife's daughter, begotten of thy father, she is thy sister, thou shall not uncover her nakedness. Thou shall not uncover the nakedness of thy father's sister; she is your father's near kinswoman. Thou shall not uncover the nakedness of thy mother's sister; for she is your near kinswoman.

The Allah that gave Prophet Mohammed the power to uncover the nakedness of his sisters, maternal aunts, brother's daughters, and any woman that is happy to open her legs is definitely not our Jehovah Jireh, who considered any canal knowledge of a near kinsperson a great abomination. With these abominable acts, Prophet Mohammed has misled millions of his followers, who engage in similar behaviours, which they regard as Islamic, to this day.

Sex and other carnal pleasures are paramount as a recruiting tool for the followers of Allah – the jihadists and mujahideen – that late author and journalist Muhammad Galal Al-Kushk wrote, "The men in Paradise have sexual relations not only with the women who are from this world and the black-eyed, but also with the serving boys." Al-kushk continued, "In Paradise, a believer's penis is eternally erect." Are you kidding me?

Now, readers, do all these texts about Islam and Mohammed sound in any way holy or godly? In Islam paradise, wine will be flowing like in a London brothel; virgins never polluted by men or demons would be wrapped up in men's bosoms; and a believer's "penis will be eternally erect." This image contrasts greatly with the teaching of Jesus Christ about paradise given in

Matthew 22: 30 as follows: "For in the resurrection they neither marry, nor are given in marriage, but are as the angels of God in heaven." You may want to ask, "What is wrong with God?" He seems to be abandoning the doctrine of Jesus Christ and adopting Mohammed's doctrine, promising a paradise wherein Allah has opened a twelve-star riverside hotel, and the eternally erect penises of the Islamic faithful shall be in the bosoms of seventy virgins. I am sure Muslims will remain busy in their paradise and will not sleep, day or night, until thy kingdom come.

Like the Bible has told us, our Lord never changes. All of these pictures of Islam that we now see, courtesy of loved ones who have deserted this evil religion through the blood of Jesus Christ, have given us a lot of insight into the evil mind-set of this satanic faith, its adherents, and its prophet. Jesus Christ was in the wilderness, fasting for forty days and nights, when Satan appeared and promised him all the good things of the world and tempted him to turn stone into bread. To the glory of Jehovah, Jesus Christ triumphed, and Satan went away in shame. Unfortunately, with all we now know about Islam, Satan found his man in Mohammed, with the promise of wealth, looting, and – most importantly – having sex with seventy virgins in Islamic paradise. Mohammed surely bowed down to Satan in the form of Allah.

No wonder the symbol of Islam is the half moon, the image dedicated to the worship of the moon god.

The Essence of Faith and Religion

To better understand the next topic, I think it is expedient to define through both social and spiritual prisms some of the terms associated with it.

"Faith", according to the English dictionary is defined as confidence or trust in a person, thing, deity, or in the doctrines or teachings of a religion. It can also be defined as belief that is not based on proof as well as confidence based on some degree of warrant. Faith is synonymous to hope, trust, and belief.

However, Hebrew 11: 1–13 gives a Christian view of faith as follows:

> Now faith is the substance of things hoped for, the evidence of things not seen. For by it the elders obtained a good report. Through faith we understand that the worlds were framed by word of God, so that things which are seen were not made of things which do appear. By faith Abel offered unto God a more excellent sacrifice than Cain, by which he obtained witness that he was righteous, God testifying of his gifts: and by it he being dead speaks. By faith Enoch was translated that he should not see death; and was not found, because God had translated him: For before his translation he had this testimony, that he pleased God. But without faith it is impossible to please Him: for him that cometh to God must believe that He is, and that He is a rewarder of those that diligently seek Him. By faith Noah, being warned of God of things not seen as yet, moved with fear, prepared an ark to the saving of his house; by which he condemned the world, and became heir of the righteousness which is by faith. By faith Abraham, when he

was called to go out into a place where he should after receive for an inheritance, obeyed; and he went out, not knowing whither he went. By faith he sojourned in the land of promise, as in a strange country, dwelling in tabernacles with Isaac and Jacob, the heirs with him of the same promise: For he looked for a city which hath foundations, whose builder and maker is God. Through faith also Sara herself received strength to conceive seed, and was delivered of a child when she was past age, because she judged Him faithful who has promised. Therefore sprang there even of one, and him as good as dead, so many as the stars of the sky in multitude, and as the sand is by sea shore innumerable. These all died in faith, not having received the promises, but having seen them afar off, and were persuaded of them, and embraced them, and confessed that they were strangers and pilgrims on the earth.

Religion is defined by the English dictionary as "An organised collection of beliefs, cultural system, and world views that relate humanity to an order of existence."

From the above definitions, it is crystal clear that religion and faith are like conjoined twins whose lives depend on one another. Whether you are Christian, Muslim, or of another faith, you will readily agree that your faith and religious affiliation can easily influence your life, your thought process, your attitude, and your behavioural pattern. It can command your allegiance to your chosen deity, including the Christian or Jewish God.

The aforementioned thought process explains why people sometimes obey religious figures without question. Unfortunately, some people go to the extreme of committing atrocious crimes against humanity like maiming, hostage taking, beheading, and mass killing in the name of their religion.

The models and messages that the leaders of religions pass down are very important in determining the conduct and behavioural patterns of their denominations. Whatever faith system controls your life absolutely controls your mind, your ego, and your personality. Sometimes you can assess the character of a religious organisation or group of individuals by their deeds. The teachings, doctrine, and character of the leader of a religious group shape the character and conduct of the followers, and this is what determines if a religion is from God or from false doctrines or Satan.

Therefore, the only litmus test we can do to determine if a religion is of God or of Satan is to observe the way its followers behave in modern society: how peacefully do they coexist with their neighbours or propagate their religion? Make no mistake: no one has ever seen God, and no one has been there when the so-called prophets of God received religious mandates, so it is practically impossible to verify their messages. But it is in our power and in the domain of common sense to determine which religion is good or bad – peaceful or dangerous – and from this determine whether it is from God Almighty. There's a saying that if it walks like a duck, swims like a duck, and quacks like a duck, then it probably is a duck. Therefore, if the modus operandi of a religion acts like it is from Satan, sounds like it is from Satan, and unleashes terror like Satan, it is from Satan. It is time to tell our Muslim fellow inhabitants of this world that the way they behave cannot convince anyone who has an atom of decency and common sense that Islam is a religion of peace from God, the creator of heaven and earth.

How do you justify killing your own daughter simply because she chooses to marry a person of another faith? And how do you explain the rationale for bombing churches full of worshippers or strapping a bomb to yourself and detonating it inside a train, plane, bus, or shopping mall amidst innocent people? If this unholy war has any signature at all, it is the signature of Satan, your father.

Christianity teaches in Matthew 5: 16 to "let your sun shine so much that people will see your good work and glorify your father who is in heaven." And Matthew 5: 14 says, "You are the salt of the earth, a city set on hill top cannot be hidden." According to 1 Corinthians 10: 27, if pagans invite you to share a meal, go and eat with them after you bless the food in the name of the Lord, and then preach to them in peace and harmony. In Luke 10: 5, Jesus Christ instructs his followers, "And any house you shall enter, say to them, peace be unto you, if they accept you, preach the word to them but if they reject you, come out of the house and shake off the dust on your sandals as a testimony to them and your peace shall go with you."

Jehovah did not give instructions to hate, kill, or behead pagans for the sake of evangelism or submission in any of these passages. However, Allah commands killings to enforce submission. In Koran 9. 123, it is written, "Oh ye who believe! Fight those of the disbelievers who are close to you, and let them find harshness in you, and know that Allah is with those who are the pious." And Koran 9. 73 says, "O prophet! Strive hard against the disbelievers and the hypocrites, and be harsh against them." Koran 2. 191 instructs, "Kill the disbelievers wherever you find them." In Koran 5. 34, we read, "Slay or crucify or cut off the hands and feet of the unbelievers, that they be expelled from the land with disgrace and that they shall have a great punishment in world hereafter." Additionally, Koran 47. 4 says, "Strike off the heads of the disbelievers, and after making a great slaughter among them, carefully tie up the remaining captives." Compare these hateful, violent, and satanic teachings of Prophet Mohammed and the Koran to the peaceful, love-filled, and productive teachings of our Lord, Jesus Christ and the Bible. This illustrates that Islam is definitely not a religion of peace but one that blows things into pieces. The essence of true religion is to bring peace, comfort, harmony, and restoration to human bodies and souls. It is only the devil and thieves that come to steal, maim, and kill (see John 10: 10).

Give glory to the true God, Jehovah. Through the blood of the saviour, he has granted mercy to millions of Muslims who are deserting their horrible faith for the light of Jesus Christ and revealing the covert danger to humanity hidden in the Koran. Not all Muslims are allowed to learn the depth of the Koran until they reach the oath of the blood, at a point in their learning of the Qur'an they must shed the blood of a fowl, goat, cow and even human, and the reasons for this are becoming more evident. If you still wonder why Muslims are so bloodthirsty, look into the teachings of their evil book and horrible prophet; you will discover that the apple does not fall far from the tree.

They are the loudest voice in calling their religion peaceful to make people unaware of their wickedness. As such, these Muslims are an example of what Proverbs 10: 18 warns against: "Whoever hides his hatred has lying lips," just like Satan, their father, who is the grand commander of lies (see John 8: 44).

It is my prayer that those who read this book will not shout for fatwa on the writer's head but – through the blood of Jesus Christ who died for their sins – will shout for Jehovah's mercy and repentance and become children of God.

Who Is God Almighty, Jehovah Jireh or Allah?

All people who believe in God know he is the Lord God Almighty, the creator of heaven and earth, and the only sovereign being who is omnipotent, omniscient, and omnipresent. We believe he is the provider for the needs of mankind the only one with power over life and death, and he will judge every person on Judgement Day, according to his or her deeds on earth. He is the honest and impartial judge who will send the righteous ones to paradise and the wicked ones to hell, where they will spend eternity after leaving this world. God is the alpha and omega – the beginning and the end – whose authority is unquestioned and whose sovereignty and rule of heaven and earth will last forever.

In the Bible, we read how God created the first couple, Adam and Eve, through his divine authority and made provision for their physical and spiritual existence. He gave them authority to nurture their beautiful garden and abode.

In Genesis 2: 7–9, we read the following:

> And the Lord God formed man of the dust of the ground, and breathed into his nostrils the breath of life; and man became a living soul. And the Lord God planted a garden eastward in Eden; and there he put the man whom he had formed. And out of the ground made the Lord God to grow every tree that is pleasant to the sight, and good for food; and the tree of life also in the midst of the garden, and the tree of knowledge of good and evil.

God not only created Adam but also, later, made a helper for him. He caused a deep sleep to fall on Adam, and then removed part of his ribs, out of which he created Eve. God became a labourer and for the people he created by planting a garden just for humans to survive. Even after the first couple disobeyed God and he sent them out of the Garden of Eden, he was still very kind and merciful unto them. In fact, he became the first fashion designer, as we see in Genesis 3: 21. "Unto Adam also and to his wife did the Lord God make coats of skins and clothed them."

Therefore, the picture painted here is of a kind, generous, and caring God. He acts this way to his creatures even when they are least worthy of it. God is not wicked or horrible. To Adam and Eve – and by extension, the whole human race including you and me – God is the creator, ground breaker, gardener, and provider. Even when humans first showed their sinful and disobedient nature, God did not show revenge or scorn. Rather, he showed he is a caring God who covered the shame of his erring creatures.

In Exodus 3: 13–15, God described himself to Moses as follows:

> And Moses said unto God, Behold, when I come unto the children of Israel, and shall say unto them, The God of your fathers has sent me unto you; and they say to me, What is His name? What shall I say unto them? And God said unto Moses, I AM THAT I AM: and he said, Thus shalt thou say unto the children of Israel, I AM hath sent me unto you. And God said moreover unto Moses, thus shall you say unto the children of Israel, The Lord God of your fathers, the God of Abraham, the God of Isaac, and the God of Jacob, has sent me to you; this is my name for ever, and this is my memorial unto all generations.

The last few lines affirm that he will not at some point change his name to Allah. And instead of showing mercy, kindness, and provision for humankind, he wouldn't change into a forceful and hateful killer who orders prophets to hack off people's necks in submission to his will.

Conversely, Allah, the god of the Muslims, sees the children of Abraham, Isaac, and Jacob as sinners and infidels who are preventing the cause of Allah. Throughout the Koran, Christians and Jews are referred to as "Ahl-Al-Kitab", meaning, "the people of the book". Allah ordered a permanent death sentence to infidels to be carried out through jihad. Koran 9. 124

says, "Believers! Wage war against such infidels, as are your neighbours, and let them find you rigorous." If the bombing and killing of Christians in Egypt, Iraq, Afghanistan, Pakistan, Sudan, Somalia, Nigeria, and so on is not a direct consequence of the evil order given by Mohammed, what is it? Koran 9. 124 also says, "Make war upon such of those to whom the scriptures have been given as believe not in Allah and have forbidden his Apostle, and profess not the professor of truth, until they pay tribute out of hand, and they be humbled."

In the massacres of Jews at Banu Qurayza, Khaibar, and others, Muslims killed over 3 million people, making Islam the second highest killer of Jews after Adolf Hitler. Even during Hitler's rule, the caliphate in the Middle East played a great role in persecuting and executing Jews.

The Baburnama, memoirs of the founder of the Mughal Empire, reveals that tens of millions of people were killed when Muslims invaded India and proudly displayed piles of decapitated human heads as trophies.

A similarly themed popular Anasheed song has the following lyrics:

We are those who built our forts out of human skulls. Which we brought from the land of the tyrant. By force and on top of the booty. Our messenger is the one who made us noble builders of glory. Our messenger is the sun of truth, who lit the face of the world.

With this shocking revelation, it would be stupid to imagine that Almighty God, the I AM THAT I AM would degenerate from the great provider we see in the Garden of Eden to a massive killer. He would not transform into Allah, whose two-edged sword represents the moon god on one side and the bloodthirsty war god on the other, cutting deep into the bone and marrow of innocent Jews, Christians, and other so-called infidels.

Do not be deceived. There is only one God who created heaven and earth, the God of Abraham, Isaac, and Jacob, and he promised his name would not change over the generations. To think that he has changed into Allah to kill his own people, the children of Abraham, Isaac, and Jacob is pure falsehood. I AM THAT I AM is God Almighty, while Allah is simply the god of war and moon worship.

Satan, the lord of hate, lies, and trickery is called in the Bible a master of disguise. We are warned in 2 Corinthians 11: 14, "And no marvel; for Satan himself is transformed into an angel of light." The Koran 24. 35–36 states thus: "Allah is the light of heaven and the earth, a likeness of His light is as a niche in which is a lamp, the lamp is in a glass, the glass is as it were a brightly shining star, lit from a blessed olive tree, neither eastern nor western, whose oil is nigh luminous though fire scarce touched it. Light upon light! Allah does guide whom He will to His light: Allah sets forth parables for men: and knows all things." And it is not a coincidence that Koran 53. 49 describes Allah as the lord of the star of Sirius. He could be the one described and warned against in Revelation 8: 10, which says, "And the third angel sounded, and there fell a great star from heaven, burning as it were a lamp, and it fell upon the third part of the rivers, and upon the fountains of waters."

Allah has given himself many names, called the 99 beautiful names of Allah. Some of them are the Most Proud One, Al-Muthakabbir, and the Lord of the Worlds, Malek-rab Al-A'lameen. Pride and arrogance are so paramount to Allah that he boasts, "Pride is my wear, supremacy is my dress, I will break anyone who vies with me, and for them I do not care, and "Glory be to the one who rightfully deserves to be called the most Proud, He is Allah."

Beloved, this self-acclaimed lord of the worlds is the devil foretold in 2 Corinthians 4: 4, "in whom the god of this world hath blinded the minds of them which believed not, lest the light of the glorious gospel of Christ, who is the image of God should shine unto them." This biblical warning is corroborated today with the fact that among all the religions of the world today – and there are thousands of them – only Islam vehemently wages war against the glorious gospel of Christ. Muslims persecute and kill Christians, attempting to betray and damage the Messiah status of our Lord Jesus Christ. And Allah, in his arrogance (the signature of Satan), promised to break anyone who vies with him (that is, Jesus Christ and Christians), because he does not care for them.

Mohammed's Reasons for Founding Islam

Jehovah created humans so that we would worship and fellowship with him and obey his commandments. God, in turn, provides for our spiritual and physical needs in this world and beyond. This fact is established in Exodus 20: 1–26. God, the creator of heaven and earth and grand designer of the universe, is self-sufficient and will never be dependent on any human, and he desires for us to adore him as a matter of choice, not compulsion.

In Exodus 20: 2–3 Jehovah said, "I am the Lord thy God, which have brought thee out of the land of Egypt, out of the house of bondage. Thou shall have no other gods before me." This is a direct reference to the descendants of Abraham, Isaac, and Jacob – the Jews and, by lineage, Jesus Christ and Christians. If we recall, God always referred to himself as the Lord of Abraham, Isaac, and Jacob and never included Ishmael in the familial lineage. This is a big issue to the Muslims, triggering feelings of rejection and enmity amongst supposed kinsmen. As described in a previous chapter, Ishmael was a child of Hagar, the Egyptian slave woman of Sarah, given to Abraham to produce a child for Sarah, who was desperate and barren. According to tradition, Ishmael could have been raised in the household of Sarah and Abraham as their legitimate son, because any child born of a slave woman to her mistress, by act of bondage, belongs to the mistress. But because of the arrogance of Hagar and her reproach towards her mistress, Sarah ordered that Hagar and her son be cast out of the household of Abraham. As aforementioned, the only household left to raise Ishmael when this happened was the people of the deserts – Arabs and Egyptians of his mother's clan.

According to God's promise, Ishmael and his family grew into a huge and prosperous tribe in the deserts called the Ishmaelite, or Midianites, according to Genesis 37: 25–28 as follows:

> And they sat down to eat bread; and they lifted up their eyes and looked, and, behold, a company of Ishmaelite came from Gilead with their camels bearing spices and balm and myrrh, going to carry it down to Egypt. And Judah said unto his brethren, what profit is it if we slain our brother, and conceal his blood? Come, and let us sell him to the Ishmaelite, and let not our hand be upon him, for he is our flesh. And his brethren were content. Then there passed by the Midianites merchantmen, and they drew and lifted up Joseph out of the pit, and sold Joseph to the Ishmaelite for twenty pieces of silver: and they brought Joseph into Egypt.

Therefore, the prosperous clan of Ishmael extended from the Arabian deserts, from where the Midianites of this story came – which we can refer to as the present-day Middle East – to Egypt. Prophet Mohammed was one of the prosperous sons from the clan of Ishmael. And like Ishmael, Mohammed inherited a multitude of idols from his ancestors, and every deity in the Arabian deserts was called Allah, as explained previously.

No matter what the circumstances might be, Ishmael has a direct blood relation to Abraham, the Jewish patriarch and father of all faith. But unlike the monotheistic Jews and Christians, the Ishmaelite were polytheists. That is, they worshipped many gods, similar to the Ancient Egyptians.

The sad thing about idol worship is that the various devotees always engage in bloodshed, human sacrifice, occultism, rituals, and destructive battles for supremacy. This, in turn, results in wanton deaths and destruction, leading to anarchy and chaos in their lands, whereas peace reigns supreme in monotheistic lands.

In AD 610, when Mohammed grew to adulthood and read the history of the Jews and Christians in the Torah and the Holy Bible, he saw the historic connections between the descendants of Isaac and Ishmael. He became angry because Ishmael was cast out of the house of his father and jealous because the house of Isaac was peaceful and because Judaism and Christianity were accepted worldwide. More troubling for Mohammed was the fact that Jesus Christ, a Jew, was a world-acclaimed Messiah when he came to die for the sins of the world and to restore those who believe in him to God the Father. Jesus Christ's popularity completely overshadowed Ishmael, and this made Mohammed more worried. He decided to do something that would bring back the memory and popularity of Ishmael and his clan.

This is where Satan, the enemy of mankind, comes in. His method of temptation is described in Matthew 4: 8–11.

> Again, the devil takes Him up into the mountain, and showed Him all the kingdoms of the world, and the glory of them; And said unto Him, All these things will I give thee, if thou wilt fall down and worship me. Then said Jesus unto him, get thee hence, Satan: for it is written, Thou shalt worship the Lord thy God, and Him only shall thou serve. Then the devil leaves Him, and, behold, angels came and minister unto Him.

Satan showed Jesus Christ these kingdoms on earth so that he would betray his father in heaven. Jokes aside, one of them must have been the kingdom of Saudi Arabia, where the prophet Mohammed ultimately came from. He inherited it after bowing to Satan and accepting the satanic job that Jesus Christ rejected.

We know that God Almighty operates in the realm of the spirit, and so does Satan. We cannot see either being in the physical realm. Hence, when Jehovah made the decision to visit mankind, he came incarnated as Jesus Christ; likewise, for Satan to operate freely, he must come in human form. This is why Satan attempted to hijack Jesus Christ, as related in the preceding passage from Matthew. If Jesus had accepted, it would have enabled Satan to stop God from saving mankind from the devil and to prevent Jehovah's ministry from reaching the darkest parts of the earth with the light of salvation.

After Satan's failure in this situation, he constantly and desperately looked for someone else to use. Remember, when the devil saw the lust for money and worldly possessions in the heart of Judas Iscariot, he was very swift in possessing him. He easily used Judas to betray Jesus Christ, thinking this would stop the gospel from spreading. We read in Luke 22: 3–4, "Then entered Satan into Judas surnamed Iscariot, being of the number of the twelve. And he went his way and communed with the chief priests and captains, how he might betray Him unto them." Do not forget that Satan has his devilish eyes on people of God, and he is bent at destroying them so that they will not be able to propagate Jehovah's cause. The affliction of Job, reducing him from grace to ashes, is another example of Satan's attempts to deceive humans and make them disobey God. Job 1: 8–9 says, "And the Lord said unto Satan, Hast thou considered my servant Job, that there is none like him in the earth, a perfect and an upright man, one that feared God, and eschewed evil? Then Satan answered the Lord, and said, Doth Job fear God for nought?" And in verse 11, Satan opined, "But put forth thine hand now, and touch all that he hath, and he will curse thee to thy face." All the destruction and devastation that Job suffered from Satan, the enemy of the soul, is clearly documented. This account shows that Satan, in his spirit form, has the power to see the contents of human hearts.

God saw the saintly spirit in Jesus Christ among the angels before choosing him as the Messiah; similarly, Satan saw the greed and lust for money in Judas Iscariot before picking him to destroy his enemy, Jesus Christ.

In the garden of Gethsemane, Satan tried frantically to stop Jesus Christ from delivering salvation to the world. He knew that if Jesus Christ succeeded in shedding his blood on the cross at Calvary, salvation and reunion with Jehovah would be available to humanity. This spelled disaster for Satan, whose kingdom on earth would be severely compromised, as described in John 1: 12 as follows: "But as many as received Him, to them He gave the power to be the sons of God, even to them that believe on His name." Satan took this message seriously and personally; his wish is to subject the world to his rule. How dare Jesus Christ even attempt to reverse his plan? But Satan failed in the garden of Gethsemane once again. When he tried to bring the fear of pain and agony of death over Jesus Christ, the power of prayers and trust in God's empowerment prevailed. We read in Luke 22: 42–43, Jesus prayed, Father, if thou be willing, remove this cup from me; nevertheless not my will, but thine be done. And there appeared an angel unto Him from heaven, strengthening Him." After Satan tried and failed, the angel of God appeared to strengthen Jesus Christ. And then Satan introduced a conspiracy theory through Islam stating that Jesus Christ was not the person killed on the cross. Rather, Allah exchanged Jesus Christ for the devil, and the latter was crucified. But when the Messiah rose on the third day, as promised, and showed his disciples the wounds on his hands and legs – as vehemently confirmed and proven by the apostle Thomas – Satan had no further conspiracy theory to put forward. The presence and actions of prominent Jews at the site in Golgotha was significant too. For example, Joseph of Arimathea volunteered a grave intended for his use as a burial site for Jesus in Mark 15: 43, which says, "Joseph of Arimathea, an honourable counsellor, which also waited for the kingdom of God, came, and went in boldly unto Pilate, and craved the body of Jesus." There was also a centurion and those with him, mentioned in Matthew 27: 50–54, as follows:

> Jesus, when he had cried again with a loud voice, yielded up the ghost. And, behold, the veil of the temple was rent in twain from top to the bottom; and the earth did quake, and the rocks rent. And the graves were opened; and many bodies of the saints which slept arose. And came out of the graves after His resurrection, and went into the holy city, and appeared unto many. Now when the centurion, and they that were with him, watching Jesus, saw the earthquake, and those things that were done, they feared greatly saying, truly this was the son of God.

The Jews never disputed the fact that Jesus was a messiah or that he would die on the cross and be resurrected on the third day. That is why the elders of the temple and the Romans urged the guards not to tell anyone that Jesus had indeed arisen. They even offered the guards money and other incentives to keep their mouths sealed on the matter. The primary issue the Jews had with Jesus was that they refused to accept that their messiah would come from the family of a commoner, an ordinary carpenter. To them, a messiah must be an important person from the upper class or some mysterious power from the sky, not a human born in a manger.

All scripture is like an infection to the essence of Satan, who will forever be unhappy that his kingdom on earth has been dealt an exterminating blow. He especially hates statements such as the one that follows from John 11: 25–26: "Jesus said unto her, I am the resurrection, and the life; he that believeth in me, though he were dead, yet shall he live. And whosoever lives and believeth in me shall never die. Believeth thou this?" Similarly, John 10: 9 says, "I am the door; by me if any man enter in, he shall be saved, and shall go in and out, and find pasture." Jesus said and did many things to demonstrate that his authority in heaven and earth, as affirmed by

Jehovah, is endless. This makes Satan, who has eternally vowed to damage the holy affirmation no matter what, suffer from a crippling headache.

Just like the devil hired Judas Iscariot he now has a new hireling in the prophet Mohammed, as foretold by Jesus Christ in John 10: 10–14 as follows (emphasis mine).

> The thief cometh not, but for to steal, and to kill, and to destroy: I am come that they might have life, and that they might have it more abundantly. I am the good shepherd; the good shepherd gives his life for the sheep. But he that is a *hireling*, and not the shepherd, whose own the sheep are not, see the wolf coming, and leaves the sheep, and flee; and the wolf catches them, and scattered the sheep. The *hireling* flees, because he is a *hireling*, and cares not for the sheep. I am the good shepherd, and know my sheep, and am known of mine. As the Father knows me, even so know I the Father; and I lay down my life for the sheep.

This topic will be explored further in the next chapter.

The Satanic Hireling

Satan's hireling, Prophet Mohammed, has surely come to steal, kill, and destroy, considering the millions of people who the sword of Allah has beheaded. You don't need to look far into any Islamic nation before you see the symbol of death, two crossing swords, proudly displayed. In Matthew 26: 25–54, we read how Jesus Christ rebuked Peter, one of His disciples, for cutting off an ear of one of the Roman guards sent to arrest him. "Then said Jesus unto him, put up again thy sword into its place, for all they that take the sword shall perish with the sword. Thinks thou that I cannot now pray to my Father, and He shall presently give me more than twelve legions of angels? But how then shall the scriptures be fulfilled, that thus it must be?" Jesus Christ even performed an undeserved miracle for his enemy by picking up the severed ear and restoring it to its place. These actions demonstrate a clear distinction between a good shepherd, who came to save all humans no matter their status, and a trigger-happy sword-wielding thief and hireling of Satan.

The destruction Muslims have carried out is astronomical. They blow up cars, trains, aeroplanes, buses, and homes on a daily basis, causing human deaths in the hundreds at the same frequency. A day never passes in Iraq, Pakistan, Syria, Afghanistan, Iran, Somalia, Kenya, Nigeria, Gaza, Yemen, the Central African Republic, Sudan, Egypt, and other parts of the world without the bloodthirsty Allah drinking human blood. Every time it's offered, his followers will happily shout, "Allah-hu-akbar!" This constant killing and persecution is destroying Christianity. Muslims warriors are taking Coptic Christians and others worldwide to the slaughterhouses of Islam for daily sacrifice on the blood-soaked altar of the moon god named Allah. The newly created and soon-to-be destroyed Islamic state between Iraq and Syria has just announced that all Christians in Mosul must either convert to Islam or face mass beheadings. Allah will soon have another ocean of human blood to drink if the good people of the world do not stop the evil caliphate and its agents.

In the early 1980s, a Christian businessman in the city of Kano in northern Nigeria, Gideon Akaluka, was beheaded simply because a peanut vendor wrapped her product in a piece of tattered Koran when she gave it to him. An Islamic thug found this man eating from the paper and screamed, "Wa-yo-Allah," which means "blasphemy". A legion of law enforcement agents could not stop the Islamic ruffians from breaking into the jail where Gideon Akaluka was being kept for his safety. They used a saw blade to sever his head from his body, thrust it onto a nomad's stick, and carried the still-dripping head in a victory parade on Kano Street after an evil Friday prayer (Jumat service). The hirelings of Satan are very good at shedding blood. I too could have been beheaded in Saudi Arabia as a foreign worker for taking a Bible written in a foreign language. However, Jehovah helped me to blind them so that they could not interpret the language. You can be jailed for receiving a Christmas card in Saudi Arabia, and Easter is never celebrated there. Every Friday after Jumat prayers, Saudis are invited to watch beheadings, where so-called blasphemers are executed by the sword or the crescent-shaped blades. The condemned are typically common criminals such as burglars or adulterers and aid workers caught with the Bible or preaching the gospel of Christ. You can see the joy in the eyes of these Muslims for the opportunity to shed blood on their lands. The half-moon-shaped weapon used in such beheadings symbolizes the rituals when humans were sacrificed to Allah, the moon god, in their dark ages. If this is not an ugly enough sight, wait until you see Saudi leaders and princes who claim to be the custodians of the two holy mosques and Kaaba dancing with the swords and wielding them vigorously as if ready to go to war. This is another confirmation that Islam belongs to Satan's hirelings, who are ever-ready to steal, kill, and destroy. No wonder Mohammed was so skilful in invading nations, killing their people, and stealing their treasures. This is the source of Mohammed's wealth and the foundation upon which Islam, Saudi Arabia, Mecca and Medina, and Kaaba were built upon.

When Satan successfully hired Mohammed to undermine of the saviour status of Jesus Christ, it created an evil collaboration to establish an Ishmaelite war machine against the other children of Abraham, Jews and Christians. Because of this evil agenda shared between Satan and Mohammed, we see a deadly combination in the world today.

It is little wonder that the loudest song the Islamists sing is, "Allah begets not, nor is Allah begotten," In other words, God has no child, and no one gave birth to Him. It is the music of the Antichrist sponsored by Lucifer, the great liar. In Matthew 3: 16–17, the Bible says, "And Jesus, when He was baptized, went up straightway out of the water; and, lo, the heavens were opened unto Him, and he saw the spirit of God descending like a dove, and lighting upon Him: And lo a voice from heaven, saying, "this is my beloved Son, in whom I am well pleased." The account in Luke 9: 35 of the transfiguration of Jesus Christ similarly says, "And came a voice out of the cloud, saying, this is my beloved Son: hear Him." These two accounts showed God openly announcing his paternity of Jesus Christ in people's hearing to rule out any molecule of doubt. However, the evil forces collaborating against Jesus Christ, specifically Satan and Mohammed, lied to their followers and claimed that Jesus Christ is not the Son of God.

The first lie Lucifer asked Mohammed to tell distorted the facts about Isaac being the promised child that Jehovah asked Abraham to sacrifice to him as a test of faith. Despite this documented fact and a period of about 3,000 years between Abraham's time and the time that Mohammed was born, Mohammed told his ignorant followers the bold-faced lie that it was Ishmael whom God asked for in sacrifice. This is the reason millions of Muslims across the globe celebrate Idl El-Adha, when they must kill rams or goats as Abraham supposedly sacrificed instead of his son Ishmael. Because this lie has been told again and again, people tend to believe it, and more so because they face the threat of amputation, beheading, or imprisonment if they dare to challenge the falsehood.

The evil duo of Satan and Mohammed simply replicates and distorts Bible stories to suit their agenda. They do this to deceive their followers and make themselves sound like they are from Jehovah. This is why they call the prophet Moses, Prophet Musa; they call the prophet Jacob, Prophet Yakub; and they call the prophet Noah, Nurudeen. They deliberately degraded Jesus Christ by calling him Prophet Issa, the son of Mariam, not the Son of God. But while the Christian Bible and Jehovah's prophets and apostles emerged before our eyes, the Koranic story and characters emerged from copycat accounts which have no relevance in modern history.

The Jamshedi Festival

One such copycat story is celebrated in Iran every year throughout the land of the mullahs and ayatollahs. It is called the Jamshedi Nowruz festival. It commemorates a time when they claim Allah was going to destroy the people of the world for their sins and terrible crimes, but he chose to spare the prophet Narus and his household for their steadfastness and honesty to Allah. According to the story, Allah told Narus to go into a cave, along with his family and choice animals: birds, plants, insects, and other creatures. As soon as Narus and his family entered the cave with their chosen animals and other treasured property, snow fell continually on the whole earth and killed plants, animals, and all other humans. This story mimics the Great Flood of the prophet Noah to make Islam look like a credible religion. However, jihadist ideology does not resemble religion. Rather, it is a politically motivated entity disguised as a religion to attract bloodthirsty and criminal-minded men to make their murderous insanity look like an act of killing for Allah. It is similar to how the Rastafarians turn their habitual cannabis smoking into a religious affiliation of peace and brotherhood. The major difference is that Rastafarians are generally peaceful people who will never kill or hurt people who don't agree with them – those who made a healthy personal choice to abhor hallucinogenic marijuana consumption.

The ninety-ninth name of Allah, Al-Darr, which literally means "The Causer of Harm, the Afflicter and Creator of all Sufferings," was manifest in the past and has been reawakened today. Mohammed killed more human beings with the sword of Allah than any other warrior in human history, and the killing machine he put in motion is still operational today. It probably will be present forever if reasonable people of this world do not stop it. Thousands of pregnant women have had their abdomens slit open and their foetuses taken out and killed by Muslims in northern Nigeria, Sudan, Iraq, Afghanistan, the Central African Republic (CAR) and other Islamic parts of the globe. In the Central African Republic, Christians had to lift guns and machetes, against commandments like turning the other cheek, to chase Muslim out of their country because they were unable to withstand the horrible death, looting, rape, and robbery. For decades, violent Muslims have hanged, slit throats, stoned to death, or imprisoned many Christian pastors, converts, and preachers. The criminal newly carved out Islamic State in the Iraq-Syria desert was so swift in killing Christians in the city of Mosul in Iraq; hundreds of thousands of people were displaced, and those who were left behind were given the ultimatum, "Accept Islam, pay tax, or be killed." The Lord God Almighty does not wear violent face. This is the face of Satan, the fallen star, and master of the prophet Mohammed. I completely agree with the ninety-ninth name of Allah. He is indeed the original causer of harm, afflicter, and creator of all suffering.

Allah is Satan, the lord of the dawn and the fallen star, as depicted by the star logo on every mosque. And the Koran proudly states, "I seek refuge with [Allah] the Lord of the Dawn from the mischief of the evil that He [Allah] has created … from the mischievous evil of Darkness as it becomes intensely dark" (Koran 114. 1–3).

Allah is also the proud Lord of the demons – called jinn in the Arab world – as revealed in Koran 51. 56: "I only created jinn [demons] and man to worship me; demons were said to have accepted Allah as their Lord after reading the Koran, as quoted in Koran 72. 13. "Since we [the demons] have listened to the guidance of the Koran, we have accepted Islam; and any who believes in his lord [Allah] has no fear of loss, force or oppression." And in Koran 72. 1–8, the demons hailed their Lord. "Say [Oh Mohammed] It is revealed unto me that a company of the jinn gave ear, and they said: Lo! It is a marvellous Koran which guides unto righteousness, so we believe in it and we ascribe unto our Lord no partner." This has the appearance of collaboration between Allah, the great Satan, and the angels with whom he fell from heaven on the Night of Destiny in Koran 97. 1–5. "We have sent it down to thee in the Night of Destiny, what do you know of this Night of Destiny? The Night of Destiny is better than a thousand months. In it, the angelic hosts descend along with the spirit by command of their Lord Allah, Peace shall it be until the rising of the Dawn [Morning Star]." The demons referred to in the preceding quotations have vowed not to ascribe any partner to their lord and Allah. Because they are mutually interested in and benefit from grief and bloodshed, it is easy for Satan and demons with the same motives to work together to fight against their single major enemy, Jesus Christ, who spent his lifetime on earth casting out demons. But Jesus Christ saw this coming. Luke 10: 18 says, "I saw Satan fall like lightening from heaven," in reference to the arrival of an evil angel, their lord mentioned in the Koranic Night of Destiny.

Enmity, rivalry, and a battle for domination have united the great liar Satan and his easily identified hireling, Prophet Mohammed. Allah and Islam camouflage a dodgy agenda of politics and warfare as a so-called religion of peace to deceive followers into using the name of God to break things into pieces. They destroy churches, and they kill and persecute Christians and anything that has to do with Jesus Christ.

And because birds of a feather flock together, it is easy for violent-minded people in prison to convert from murderers, robbers, rapists, or drug addicts into followers of Islam. After all, they can comfortably continue to do many evil things in the name of Allah. And when they die as mujahedeen, they will go to Islamic paradise where, according to their sheiks and mullahs, Islamic rogues and martyrs will have sex with seventy virgins daily because "in paradise, the believer's penis is constantly erect."

Who Is Truly Sent by God Almighty, Jesus Christ or Prophet Mohammed?

Before we can understand who the messenger is, it would be wise to know who the sender is. In this context, it is God Almighty, the creator of and provider for all humankind, plants, and animals. He is the owner of the hills and mountains and the one who replenishes oceans, rivers, springs, brooks, and waterfalls. He has no beginning or end, and his wisdom needs no advisor or committee. He is the life that gives lives, the soul that manufactures souls, the breath that manufactures breaths, and the one who nurtures from womb to grave. He provides for the elephant and the ant in the same jungle, the whale and the shrimp in the same ocean, and the man and the sparrow in the same neighbourhood.

In John 4: 24, Jesus Christ explains, "God is spirit; and they that worship Him must worship Him in spirit and in truth." And James 1: 17 informs us that "every good gift and every perfect gift is from above, and cometh down from the Father of lights, with whom is no variableness, neither shadow of turning." These Bible passages, among many others, reveal Jehovah as a God who is pure, perfect, and good. He is the Father of lights and the source of purity; he lives in heaven and gives good and perfect gifts to the world. He sends rain in its own time to nurture the field and grow the crops; he also sends good air for man and animals to breathe and therefore survive; he gives us sunshine for light, which makes plants germinate. He also made a body of water for fish; forests for animals that roam; earth for the ants, crickets, and other animals which burrows; and the sky for birds. The Lord God is good all the time, and everything he has done is good. Genesis 1: 29–31 describes this as follows:

And God said, Behold, I have given you every herbs bearing seed, which is upon the face of all the earth, and every tree, in the which is the fruit of a tree yielding seed; to you it shall be for meat. And to every beast of the earth, and to every fowl of the air, and to everything that creeps upon the earth, wherein there is life, I have given every herb for meat; and it was so. And God saw everything that He had made, and, behold, it was very good. And the evening and the morning were the sixth day.

This God could never be party or agent to anything that is objectively destructive. Likewise, a good God would never employ a harmful messenger.

Jesus Christ came simply to do the will of his father – to die as a sacrifice for the sins of many to restore humankind to God after the fall in the Garden of Eden. Romans 5: 12–15 says the following:

Wherefore, as by one man sin entered the world, and by sin; and so death passed upon all men, for that all have sinned: (For until the law sin was in the world: but sin is not imputed when there is no law. Nevertheless death reigned from Adam to Moses, even over them that had not sinned after the similitude of Adam's transgression, who is the figure of him that was to come. But not as the offence, so also is the free gift. For if through the offence of one many be dead, much more the grace of God, and the gift by grace, which is by one man Jesus Christ, hath abounded unto many.)

Therefore, Jesus Christ was humbly qualified to say, "I have done thy will, my God." This demonstrates to the whole world and the heavens that Jesus Christ is the good shepherd, the messenger sent by the only true God. For this reason, "God has exalted Him above any other name that in the name of Jesus Christ every knee shall bow and every tongue confess that Jesus Christ is Lord to the glory of God the Father" (Phil. 2: 10). This is one major reason Satan and his hirelings have vowed to destroy any victories of the Lord Jesus Christ and to keep the kingdom of God from propagating. Instead of bowing to confess the name and power of the Lord Jesus Christ, Satan hired a multitude of liars to disrespect and blaspheme the gospel of eternal salvation. But the facts speak for themselves; Jesus Christ made the blind see, made the lame and paralytic walk, and made the lepers clean. He redeemed sinners, healed broken-hearted people, opened deaf ears, and raised the dead. He received no personal gain or monetary gain; in contrast to followers of Islam, Jesus and his followers did not carry out a single instance of looting, stealing, raping, or confiscation. The Messiah's teaching has always followed the message of Matthew 10: 8, which says, "Heal the sick, cleanse the lepers, raise the dead, cast out devils: Freely you have received, freely give." In the utmost demonstration of love to mankind, he gave his life on the cross. He forgave people and taught his followers to do the same. When the Jewish leaders brought him an adulterous woman to hear his judgement, instead of ordering her stoning or beheading, he simply quipped, "He who is without sin among you, let him cast the first stone." His actions are very unlike those of the bloodthirsty Satan worshipers that chop off people's heads according to Sharia, and they even ask people to relax and watch their barbarity like a movie. Surely these mujahedeen have no human souls; they must be the jinni of a man that Satan created. The following words of Jesus Christ rightly apply to Islam and the jihadists: "You are of your father the devil, and the lust of your father you will do. He was a murderer from the beginning, and abode not in truth, because there is no truth in him. When he speaks a lie, he speaks of his own; for he is a liar, and the father of it" (John 8: 44).

Now, can the same God that made the eye order it to be gorged out of its socket? Would he who made the arm ask for it to be chopped off? Could he who made a woman conceive order the foetus to be violently sliced out of the womb while the mother is still alive, or would the designer of the human skull ask for a sword-bearer to cut it off? The answer to all these questions is no.

The people killed senselessly were the same ones that Jesus Christ died for. Therefore, the individuals killing them are the thieves hired by Satan to steal, maim, and kill; they are not the good shepherd.

Now, the devil is the great persecutor of the saints, and he has no concern for humanity. Similarly, the great crusaders against Christ are eternally determined to wipe off everything that has to do with Jesus Christ from the face of the map. They derive comfort and delight from spilling the blood of Christians on the altar and shrine of Lucifer, who changed his name to Allah. Their religion, Islam, mimics everything that is biblical just to confuse people into thinking they worship the same God, Jehovah. But this is simply a trick to create a sense of confusion to trick people into accepting their religion which ordinarily could not have a place in a decent human gathering. The sayings of Jesus Christ that by their fruits you shall know them and that no bad tree can bear good fruit are direct warning about this religion of killing. That is why some confused Muslims who cannot comprehend how a religion that claims to be of peace and from God could advocate for shedding an ocean of human blood and destroying property are trying to distance themselves from their faith. They say terrorists and be headers are not real Muslims or good ones, but the fact revealed by centuries of history is that killing, beheading, looting, taking bounty, raping, enslaving, and robbing are all acts of the prophet Mohammed, and his followers must do the same. Followers tend to emulate and internalize what they see, hear, and read from their leaders. Have you ever wondered why Muslims don't keep dogs as pets but love to keep cats? It is simply because Mohammed had cats as pets but hated dogs. Someone who spent his entire adult life hunting and laying ambushes to kill other people and loot their properties will not choose noisy dogs as pets; however, if a cat meows in the backyard during an ambush, the victim will not hear the danger coming. So, saying that only bad Muslims chop off people's heads is a lie that this religion permits to sell the faith. The two Nigerian-British Muslims that beheaded a British soldier in broad daylight on a London street did not do something that would make the prophet Mohammed ashamed. The prophet himself beheaded more innocent people than anyone in human history. So, rather than finding excuses for the bad fruit that their bad tree Islam bears, they should abandon the religion en masse and convert to Christianity. This religion believes in forgiveness and second chances for sinners, as demonstrated by Jesus Christ. He did not order beheading for the harlot brought to him; rather, he offered repentance and a perfect place in paradise. To think that Jehovah, who told us not to commit adultery, would open adultery shops in paradise, where people who were killers and murderers on earth have sex with seventy virgins a day is idiotic propaganda. Trust me: God would not allow constantly erect penises in His Holy abode, contrary to what the Islamic scholars make their mujahideen and martyrs falsely believe. They simply use this ploy to recruit able-bodied men to join Islam's killing machine.

Therefore, it is clear who is the messenger sent by God and who is the one sent by Satan. In Sudan, followers of Islam have sentenced a pregnant woman to death for marrying a Christian and abandoning Islam; in Pakistan, women have been shot under their veils while other Muslims watch and praise Allah. A female student, Malala Yousafzai, was shot in the head for going to school, and three hundred female students in Nigeria were kidnapped because they were receiving Western education. These evil actions clearly represent a religion propagated by a satanic messenger.

God's power over sinners is the opportunity he will have to determine their faith on the day of judgement. No person can escape what God decides, no matter whether the reward for their works on earth is good or bad. In God's court, there is no lawyer to distort the facts and make the innocent seem guilty, or vice versa. Revelation 22: 11–13 tells us, "He that is unjust, let him be unjust still: and he which is filthy, let him be filthy still: and he that is righteous, let him be righteous still: and he that is holy, let him be holy still. And, behold, I come quick and my reward with me, to give every man according as his work shall be. I am Alpha and Omega, the beginning and the end, the first and the last." This does not sound like an ultimate judge who wants people to help him dish out severe punishment on earth by beheading or hanging the supposed guilty parties in his name. Unlike the Satanic enforcers of Sharia, God gives sinners the opportunity to change their course and get into paradise. This is why God sent Jesus Christ to die for sinners, but Satan and his method, Sharia, will quickly chop off the heads of sinners so that they have no second chance to gain paradise. In fact, Satan does not want people in paradise, so he uses Islam to execute sinners before they get this second chance. This way, the kingdom of Satan (hell) will have a swollen population by stealing followers of Jesus.

Beheadings and blood sacrifices are customary for Islam's god of the moon, as symbolized by the crescent sign on mosques. Muslim worship of Lucifer, the fallen star, is represented by the star sign tucked into the crescent. After the 9/11 attacks and the infamous shouts of "Allah Akbar" from the murderous hijackers, I questioned why killing innocent people that God created in love and in his own image was an appropriate situation for proclaiming God – or Allah – is great. One day, the God of the Bible opened my eyes to the following words: "These things have I spoken unto you, that you shall not be offended. They shall put you out of the synagogues; yea the time cometh, that whosoever killed you will think he does God service" (John 16: 1–2). I took it as a warning that Lucifer would hire Mohammed to sell Islam as a religion of God. Muslim leaders would deceive their followers and mujahideen that beheading and killing innocent people, especially Christians, is an act of service to God.

The Bible also warns us about Islam's violent method of operation in Revelation 20: 4 (emphasis mine). "And I saw thrones, and they sat upon them, and judgement was given unto them: and I saw the *souls* of them that were *beheaded* for *witness* of *Jesus*, and the *word of God*, and which had not worshipped the beast, neither his image, neither has received his mark upon their foreheads; or in their hands; and they lived and reigned with Christ a thousand years."

Why does Islam still glorify beheadings, when few other religions do, if any, in today's society? It is the hallmark of Lucifer and of his satanic religion; even atheists and other idol worshippers don't sever human heads like Islam teaches. Their prime targets are Christians and saints. Their leader is the beast, Satan. The black patches on the foreheads of Muslims result from constantly hitting their foreheads on the floor when worshipping their idols, and the mark on their hands is from the counting beads for prayers and the swords that they hold. No ceremonial occasion or festival in a Muslim nation is complete without the leaders celebrating the sword – the tool Satan gave them to chop off the heads of the saints. The Bible is clear on followers of Islam: By their fruits, you shall know them (see Matt. 7: 20).

Mohammed, the bloodthirsty Satanic leader, gloated at the beheading of a so-called enemy when Abdullah, a caliph, cut off Abba Hakam's head and carried it to his master. He said, "The head of the enemy of Allah!"

Mohammed joyfully exclaimed, "Allah! There is no other god but him!"

Abdullah replied, "Yeah! There is no other!" He cast the freshly severed head at the feet of the prophet. In AD 627, Mohammed besieged the Jewish village of Qurayza. After the initial massacre, the prophet of the "ever-merciful" Allah ordered the beheading of thousands of men, women, boys, girls, and babies and then buried them in trenches. In a jihad, the victims' heads must be chopped off even if they are dead. Muslims appear to love damaging heads and skulls. A popular Muslim, Sheikh Qaradawi, states Mohammed's will on Judgement Day as follows: "Ya Muslim [O Muslim], Ya Abd-Allah [O slaves of Allah], Hatha Yhudi [here is a Jew].

Ta'ala waqta' ra'sah [come and chop off his head]." Muslim countries all over the world put satanic graffiti on their walls that says things such as, "We knock on the gates of heaven with the skulls of Jews." Jews and Christians are the people of Jehovah whom Lucifer, the Muslim god, is out to destroy so that the work of salvation and redemption is stopped.

Andrew Boston, an editor of *The Legacy of Jihad* revealed the sick psyche of Babur, the founder of Mughal Empire in the fifteenth century, stating that he defeated his so-called infidel enemies as follows: "Those who were brought in alive [after surrender] were ordered beheaded, after which a tower of skulls was erected in the camp."

If a Muslim tells you that Islam is a religion of peace and that it is from God, give the person a mirror and ask him or her to look at the reflection and tell you what he or she sees.

And this value for killing is passed from generation to generation of Muslims. In fact, Muslim students in Birmingham and across the United Kingdom have access to a syllabus teaching them how to carry out holy beheadings. After all, Muslim males are mujahedeen and must chop off heads until the whole world bows down to their beast.

In August 2014, the whole world was shocked when members of the Yazidi tribe in Iraq and other minorities, including Christians, were abducted. The women were taken as sex slaves to satisfy the horrible and criminal sexual drives of the ISIS mujahedeen. The so-called merciful and beneficent Allah sent jihadists to bury five hundred women and children while they were still mostly alive and to crucify men in the scorching heat of the Iraqi desert. Those that fled to the mountains near Sinja were systematically and "beneficently" killed. The properties, flocks, money, and other possessions left behind were shared among the Islamic pack of wolves, characteristic of Mohammed's style. On a YouTube video, the father of an eight-year-old boy who held the severed head of an Iraqi soldier congratulated his son, saying, "That is my boy." The sight was so disturbing that the American secretary of state, John Kerry, described it as appalling.

John Kerry failed to realize that the prophet Mohammed looking from his hell and corroborating the statement of the boy's father by saying, "Oh, yes! He is my boy – another member of the mujahedeen." The boy demonstrated what Mohammed expects his followers to do. Even though Jesus Christ wants no one to keep the little ones from coming to him, this child holding another human's severed head is not in this group. Unless Islam is a religion of the devil, how do we explain fighters kneeling down in unison to pray to Allah after chopping off human heads, reminiscent of the pagan rituals in the pre-Islamic Arabian desert? They simply continue their satanic worship camouflaged as worship of God, and every Friday in the compound of the holiest mosques in Saudi Arabia, human sacrifices and beheadings take place. Before the blood-sucking ritual, the holy executioner will aggressively wield his blade in front of the human sacrificial lamb and chant "Bismallah," meaning, "In the Name of Allah", while others say, "Yah Allah" (Oh Allah). When the blade starts cutting through the victim's neck, the spectating Muslims will shout, "Allah Akbar," meaning "God is great".

And while the world is angry with the crimes ISIS commits against humanity – which should mean "Islamic State for Immorality and Savagery", Allah and his hireling Mohammed are happy with their killer agents, enjoying every drop of human blood shed for them. Over the past two decades, the Saudis have successfully decapitated over 1,100 people for crimes ranging from drug trafficking, witchcraft, apostasy, and possession of the Bible. In the year 2003 the Saudi government beheaded fifty-two men and one woman.

It was Allah who ordered British jihadist John the Beheader to cut off the head of American journalist James Foley and show his agony on a YouTube video.

It was also Allah who ordered killings, imprisonment, and beheadings of Christian converts in Baghdad, location of the former Babylonian Empire. Reverend Andrew, a.k.a. the Vicar of Baghdad, reported that he saw a child he had recently baptised cut in half. This is a stark warning that Islam, a religion that allows a human being to be cut in half like a fish, could never be from Jehovah; it must be from Satan, the father of barbarity.

In the late fifteenth century, Babur, who founded the Mughal Empire, boasted about defeating his infidel enemies. He said, "Those who were brought in alive after surrender were ordered beheaded and a tower of skulls was erected in the camp." During that Islamic expedition in India, it is estimated that 80 million people including babies, pregnant women, and the elderly were slain. In 1842, Afghan mujahedeen took over a British garrison in Kabul and beheaded more than 2,000 men, women, and children placing their severed heads on sticks all over town as decorations. In 1980, Afghan mujahedeen beheaded 3,000 Soviet troops and used their skulls to decorate their town centres. In the Islamic world, it is popular to honour and reward those who are skilful at beheading by sending them on holy pilgrimages to Mecca, the seat of Satan on earth. Islam and blood are synonymous, whether animal, human, or both – even in the twenty-first century. In the Islamic world, billions of animals must be killed yearly, the majority in Kaaba during Hajj. While Christianity uses the blood of Jesus for the atonement of sins, Islam uses daily human or animal blood to appease their pagan god, Allah. To graduate from one facet of training in the Koran to the next, you must sacrifice an animal in blood ritual. Those who feed Allah's thirst with blood every day make him happy.

Who Is The Promised Child God Asked Abraham To Sacrifice; Isaac or Ishmael?

In previous chapters, we have discussed that Islam tells a modified version of Abraham's sacrifice and test of faith. God's covenant with special individuals does not come cheap; they must possess special values, virtues, and character traits which set them apart from their contemporaries.

God's covenant with Adam and Eve quickly broke down because they were quick to submit to the trick of Satan, the enemy of the human soul, as we read in Genesis 3. In Genesis 4, God's relationship with Cain broke down because he was jealous and callous enough to kill his brother Abel, who was steadfast before God and honouring God with his possessions. Cain had equal opportunity to please Jehovah by offering healthy produce in sacrifice, but he chose rotten and blemished farm products. Abel, in contrast, chose his best fatted ram to sacrifice to God. So while Abel became the first man to offer an acceptable sacrifice to God, Cain became the first murderer in the human race.

In Genesis chapters 7 and 8, we read about Noah, who was credible and amiable before God. Noah and his household were the only people whom God would spare during the destruction of the earth. The people in his time were murderous, treacherous, and filthy in all their ways, but Noah and his family were honourable men and women without blemish before God.

Genesis 9: 1 says, "And God blessed Noah and his sons, and said unto them, be fruitful, and multiply, and replenish the earth." God always rewards upright people very handsomely. The blessing of Abraham is not an exception; his dedication to serving God and serving humanity gave him high moral and spiritual value before Jehovah. The same is true of Jesus Christ, whose unrivalled and clear service to God demonstrated his messiah status after his immeasurably valuable sacrifice.

God always ask for a deep relationship with honest, righteous, and humane people whose saintly living is unrivalled; those who love Jehovah God would not even hurt a fly, not to mention behead fellow humans. Rather, they are ready to lay down their own lives to save others. Their blood is priceless, and their sacrifices are dear before Jehovah.

Just like God asks for sacrifices from His devotees, so also Lucifer ask for sacrifices, but it is expedient for humans to be able to distinguish the two.

In Genesis 22: 7–14, Jehovah asked Abraham to sacrifice his dear son Isaac as a test of faith. Because Abraham did not deny God his only child, God replaced Isaac with a ram. And because Lucifer is the master of trickery and lies, more than 3,000 years after this took place with Abraham, Satan (camouflaged as Allah) hired the prophet Mohammed to deceive the world. The distorted story is that Allah asked Abraham (camouflaged as Ibrahim) to sacrifice Ishmael, the slave child, as a sacrifice of faith. No one in the world is bold enough to challenge this falsehood. The fact remains that in the days of Abraham and Isaac, there was no Islam and no Mohammed. There was only Satan, who was looking into the future for a hireling to sell his Antichrist message. Finally, he found his man in the prophet Mohammed. Ishmael's ancestry is of slave blood, with blemish inherited from his mother, the arrogant husband snatcher. Since God rejected rotten vegetables from Cain but accepted a perfect fatted animal from Abel, he would never ask for blemish from Abraham in the form of Ishmael; rather, he asked for the promised and treasured child, Isaac. Satan is simply a pathological liar telling the cooked-up story of Ibrahim and Ishmael.

Other Lies Mohammed Told the World

To spread the cause of Islam and lure its followers into the evil ideology it preaches, Satan allows Muslim zealots to deceive people into believing that Islam is the only way that leads to God. They cajole and distract innocent people into following their false doctrines. Muslims reassure themselves that the lies they tell and atrocities they commit aimed towards bringing people into the kingdom of Allah are perfectly all right.

Allah refers to himself as "Khayrul-Makireen", meaning "the greatest of all deceivers and conspirators" in Koran 3. 54, 8. 30, 50. 32, and all over the Koran. Now that the true colours of Islam are visible, we know that Allah is nothing but the same Satan who lied to the first couple in the Garden of Eden in conspiracy against Jehovah. The first part of Koran 3. 54 says, And they conspired, Allah also conspired, for he is the greatest of all deceivers." In Arabic, the word "Makara" is interpreted as "to deceive", a permissible act in Islam inasmuch as the lies, conspiracy, and scheming are to drag or force people to the cause of Allah.

In 2 John 1: 7, the Bible says, "For many deceivers are come into the world, who confess not that Jesus Christ is come in the flesh. This is the deceiver and the Antichrist." The only way you can keep people from believing the truth is to discredit it and lie repeatedly until they become so confused and convinced that the deception is actually the truth. Therefore, Islam has been lying by saying that Jesus Christ is not the Son of God and that Allah does not beget and is not begotten to deliberately discredit the truth. As aforementioned, Islam lied, saying that God actually nailed Satan to the cross instead of Jesus Christ because God loved his son and made Satan bear his agony and death. Through the Koran, Islam used this story to discredit the reality of human salvation through the shedding of the precious blood of Jesus Christ and the pain he bore for our sins. This also confused people and convinced them to believe that Jesus Christ did not die for their sins. This is Satan's agenda, carried out under his disguise as Allah and propagated by his hireling Mohammed. Their followers, the Muslims, believe it.

Muslim pilgrims are persuaded to visit the Black Stone so they can feel of the power of Allah. They point towards the stone, and they can supposedly taste it when they touch their tongue. Pilgrims circle around this magical stone held to the wall by a silver metal shaped like an oval, which some Muslims believe was placed there by Prophet Mohammed. Islam believes that the stone fell from the skies to show Adam where to build the first temple on earth. Some say it was part of a Hindu stone idol confiscated by Mohammed after invading Kaaba and killing all the infidels; others say it used to be a Hindu symbol of the goddess of fertility, because its oval shape resembles female genitalia. The fact remains that the stone has been worshipped as one of more than 360 idols in Kaaba for thousands of years. These objects of worship predate Mohammed and Islam, appearing when an Indian emperor ruled the Arabian Peninsula and brought various Hindu gods and goddesses of the moon, sun, fertility, war, and so on.

Most of these historical facts and speculations cannot be verified, but we know that the biblical account contradicts the falsehood Mohammed sold to his adherents in Islam. According to the aforementioned Muslim story, the stone fell from heaven to show Adam where to build a temple. However, in the Genesis account, Adam was cast out of the presence of the Lord God after eating the forbidden fruit with Eve, his wife. They were declared not worthy to fellowship with Jehovah anymore, and God never asked them to build him a temple. God even placed cherub an angel with a flaming sword to guard the gate leading into the Garden of Eden so that the first couple could not sneak back inside. Six thousand years later, Mohammed spread the idea of a stone falling from the sky to show a different Adam, also castaway, where to build a temple. This version cannot be anything but a satanic falsehood. Moreover, AD 620 was not an age when stones fell from the sky. This leaves us with the option that a Hindu god or goddess of fertility has been converted into use for the worship of Allah. It's little wonder that the demons declared their allegiance to Allah; after all, they recognized him as a demon chief with whom they could collaborate with to wage war on Jesus Christ. The Son of

God spent his entire life on earth casting evil spirits out of the people they possessed and afflicted. One example of this took place in the Gadarenes, where Jesus Christ healed a lunatic man by sending a legion of demons into nearby swine. The demons were so angry and disappointed by the pigs for allowing the demons to enter them instead of entering the people nearby to afflict them. The demons would have been happier to enter a million lunatics to create more suffering. This made demons and their agents hate pigs, so now I understand why Muslims hate pigs. Remember, Allah is the creator of mischief, evil men, and demons. This is why Muslims seek refuge in what the Koran calls "Rabul-Falaq", meaning "the lord of the dawn". According to Koran 114. 1–3, even Allah is so in love with evil spirits that he swears by them. And in Koran 79. 1, we read, "I swear by those who violently tear out and destroy souls." The simple reason for this is that he does it because he created them and knew them as his agents of mass destruction.

So, when a suicide bomber detonates his or her explosive device, tearing out the hearts, bodies, and souls of the innocent, unlucky bystanders and ripping them into torn metal and flesh, one cannot help but remember the collaboration between Allah and his evil forces. They love to shed blood and cause human grief. And if you are not yet convinced, ask yourself why it is considered honourable for criminals in prisons across the globe to be drawn to Islam and to easily accept it as their religion. The answer is simple: the evil spirit in them is also in Islam. That is, they learn that you can go to Muslim paradise and have sex with seventy virgins every day if you do evil things including: bank robbery; fight a jihad; hate Jews, kill Christians, and people that refuse to imbibe the evil doctrines of Islam; rape their women and daughters; steal their hard-earned property as spoils of war; cut human beings into two equal parts while they are alive; behead people like aid workers, journalists, and humanitarian officers no matter how good their intensions may be; and put bombs in your shoes, pants, or concealed in your dead baby to blow up aeroplanes and cause the mass destruction of innocent people. No recruits will do better than career criminals because the same evil that lives in them is found in Islam. Matthew 12: 24 and Ephesians 6: 12, respectively, warn of "the prince of the devils" and "rulers of the darkness of this world" in reference to Islam and Allah.

Now listen to another lie told by the prophet Mohammed to cause dissention and confusion in the region where our saviour, Jesus Christ, lived and ministered. There is a mosque in Jerusalem called Al-Aqsa mosque, and the Muslims claim it is the point where Mohammed ascended to heaven. This mosque has been idolized so much that they are ready to lay down their lives to protect it, as in their confession, "We shall shed our blood to defend our prophets and religion." There are many accounts that support the fact that our Lord and Saviour, Jesus Christ, ascended into heaven. This is confirmed by his reappearances to his disciples, the Roman guards, people on the streets, and the transfiguration of Jesus Christ. In contrast, not a single iota of evidence has emerged about the so-called glorious ascension of the prophet Mohammed into heaven from Al-Aqsa mosque, despite intense research by religious biographers and archaeologists. Even with this lack of proof, Muslims across the globe hold tight to claims that their prophet ascended from this mosque. The reason for this false claim is simple. It is a ploy of Satan to rival the holy, authentic ascension of Jesus Christ after completing his work of salvation. By doing this, Mohammedans more recent leaders can create a false legitimacy for Islam as if it were from the same God of the Christians and Jews, the founder of the world. They also wish to cause lots of confusion and deception. They know that repeating lies will eventually convince people that Islam is a religion from God. The Al-Aqsa fake story also exists for Muslims to cause chaos in the birthplace of Christianity and dominate the country, just like they have dominated other nations, such as Egypt, Syria, Sudan, Ethiopia, Lebanon, Jordan and others which were formerly Christian. Unfortunately for them, the Saudis are very sceptical of this unfounded hypothesis and have refused to throw their weight behind what could be a false claim for fear of diverting attention away from the significance of Saudi Arabia in Islam and their guardianship of the two holy mosques and the Kaaba. The Iranians and other sects in the Islamic world who share ideologies different from Wahhabism are looking for a rallying point other than Mecca and Medina. They are also trying to support Hamas in its bid to destroy Israel as vehemently avowed by the former Iranian president Ahmadinejad. These groups desire to make the Al-Aqsa Mosque their new gathering place like Mecca and Medina combined, but the Saudi princes of the clan of Mohammed are not ready to share their glory, fame, and wealth with any dissident groups. Moreover, of the large amount of foreign currencies that pours into the city of Mecca during the yearly pilgrimage

(Hajj) and lesser pilgrimage (Umrah) keeps the princes of Allah on their throne in Mecca. They will never abdicate their throne for any rabid dogs of the Islamic world like Hamas or Ahmadinejad. So, whenever Hamas kidnaps and beheads innocent Israeli citizens and deliberately fires missiles into Israel to kill citizens and provoke war, the Saudis are more than happy to look the other way. They pay little attention when the Israeli military power hits the houses of women and children in Gaza, despite the fact that Hamas activists deliberately point rockets into their civilian population to cause so-called martyrdom and to force other Islamic nations to come fight with the army of Islam to destroy Israel. Saudi Arabia is a close ally of America and Israel, the two most avowed representatives of the great Satan and eternal enemies of Islam. Who would blame the Saudis for taking such a bold stand? America provides internal and external security for the Saudis and allows them to maintain their superpower status. Otherwise, the ideological Islamists and jihadists would have completely destroyed Saudi Arabia, as evidenced in the war Osama Bin Laden waged against his own country before agents of the United States killed him.

The Islamist claim that Jerusalem belongs to them is complete nonsense; Islam has no place in the heart of the Christian Holy Land. Palestine has never been a Muslim nation. Rather, the area belongs to the people the Bible refers to as "uncircumcised Philistines" They were born pagans and idol worshippers, not Muslims, and the battle for the Biblical land of Canaan promised to the Israelites by Jehovah has been going on since the beginning of time. At one point, the Philistines – now called Palestinians – terrorized the Israelites with the giant Goliath. At another time, under Samson – the strongest Nazarene that ever lived – dominated the so-called uncircumcised Philistines. Most people have read the biblical account of Delilah, the Palestine harlot whom Palestine rulers used to entrap Samson and discover the source of his unbeatable power. The battle between David, the boy shepherd, and Goliath, a champion with the army of the Philistines, remains on record to this day. David won the battle for the army of God and killed the Goliath in battle. These stories demonstrate that the battle for land and domination between these two nations is a generational one that existed before the struggle between Jews and Muslims or Christians and Muslims. It is a battle for survival between people of God and pagans.

Muslims are circumcised by tradition, so they are not the original biblical Philistines, but the land in contest remains that of the old Philistines, now Palestine. How did the entire Palestinian nation become an Islamic nation? When an Islamic military defeated Christian and Jewish nations, the Palestinian idol worshippers easily accepted Islam to fight their common enemies, Israel and Jesus Christ. Islam stated that Jesus Christ is not the Son of God and that Allah wants his followers to destroy Jews – the people to whom God gave the Philistines' land [the Biblical land of Canaan]; no alliance could have been more compatible between those who were against the Jews. Moreover, the principalities and powers of darkness – the evil spirits in the original pagan worship of the Philistine ancestors – swore allegiance to Allah. The transition from uncircumcised paganism to circumcised Islamism was made easy from the pit of hell.

Therefore, picking a location such as Al-Aqsa mosque in the heart of the Promised Land to be the controversial spot of the disappearance of Prophet Mohammed into heaven was easily fabricated. They needed it to serve as a convergent point for jihadists all over the Muslim world to help wage war against the Israelites, so they could reclaim the old land of the Philistines for political and ideological reasons. The Saudis are not buying it, though. Let us use a little common sense and logical judgement. Mohammed walked the earth during an age modern enough that the idea of someone disappearing into heaven would be nonsensical. What's more, the ocean of human blood that prophet Mohammed shed in his lifetime through many cruel acts is not a good record for someone who would ascend alive to heaven from anywhere in the world, either Al-Aqsa or Medina. The activities of the followers of Mohammed unfolding before our eyes now do not portray the religion of a certain other man that lived and ascended into heaven life.

In the accounts we have of people ascending to heaven, they are people of good character and spirituality with behaviours that please Jehovah God, not rapists, murderers, or haters. If you read the stories of Enoch, Elijah, and Jesus Christ all that ascended live into heaven, none of them spent days and nights with carnal women and sexual immoralities, robberies, lootings, or beheadings. When did God start rewarding bad behaviours by allowing evil doers to ride on the back of flaming chariots to heaven after saying that the eyes of evildoers shall not see his glory and majesty?

Islam is a political movement rather than a religion; Muslims find it hard to separate mosque from state, they always will. The sole purpose of Islam is to rally people together in war, brainwashing them into believing they are fighting for a deity whom they are made to believe is God. Mohammed used jihadists to fight wars and amass wealth. These warriors believed that an attack on one Muslim or Muslim nation is an attack on Islam worthy of massacring innocent people. This mind-set remains a brilliant war tactic for Islam to this day.

After Friday prayers, it is easier for an imam to deploy jihadists to march against a neighbourhood or individuals to commit mass killings than for the imam to go. The jihadist can leave the comfort of Great Britain or America – riddled with fast food joints – and become a suicide bomber fighting for the cause of Islam in the God-forsaken terrain of Pakistan, Iraq, or Afghanistan. The Islamic State, on the borders of Iraq and Syria, is a place where Christians are beheaded; it is considered by some to be the ideal state for all Muslims. Jihadists obey the call to fight like zombies. With no questions asked, they jump into the line of fire like colonies of penguins jumping into a body of water after their leader took the first leap.

Who Is Allah: Ever-Loving
God or Blood-Thirsty Idol?

Every prayer in the Koran starts with "Bismallah Rahman Al Raheem" meaning, "I start in the name of Allah, the most merciful and the most beneficent."

This slogan indicates what we expect in Islam, mercy and benevolence. Allah is expected to be kind-hearted and forgiving, ever tolerant and receptive – one whose eyes of mercy shine across the globe or, simply put, who cannot hurt a fly. However, since the proof of eating is in the pudding, Islam has left a horrible taste in our mouths since its introduction in about 650 AD. The supposed religion of peace, as mentioned previously, is only a religion that breaks things into pieces. The holy book of Islam, meant to be a guide to decency and humanity, preaches only hate, killing, maiming, intolerance, and barbarity as engraved in Sharia. I was appalled to see the way Islam treats women; they are placed in the background of events in life, and they receive no family inheritance. Whilst Christianity preaches for husbands to be respectful and kind-hearted to their wives and to be ready to sacrifice everything they have for their wives, even as Jesus Christ laid down His life for the church (Eph. 5), Islam prescribes the amount of cane lashes with which a husband can beat or hit his wife, depending on the severity of her "crime". Like the saying says, it takes two to tango, but in Islam, every case of adultery ends with the woman being guilty, which is punishable by death, often by a shot to the head. In Afghan, a football stadium was converted into a shooting range for executing women. Sharia law also allows men to punish women who refused to cover their bodies head to toe by raping them. In Egypt, women were raped at public rallies or protests, including foreign journalists. When a woman was raped in Tahrir

Square in 2014, it caused an international uproar, and President Al-Sisi was forced to act. However, no rapist was ever brought to justice, simply because Islam condemns the woman for precipitating the rape. Simply put, rape is considered a permissible weapon of Allah if used to punish a woman who refused to dress modestly.

Only in Islam is there honour in killing. As another illustration of this, a father and mother will announce a fatwa on the head of their biological daughter for not marrying a Muslim or for marrying a Muslim that is not of their sect. The penalty could be stoning their daughter to death, with the father throwing the first rock. We have heard of women buried alive in Islamic countries, and even in the United Kingdom, parents have beheaded their daughters for being Western. Similarly, an American Muslim couple put their two daughters in a car, drove onto a bridge, locked in the girls inside the car, and pushed the car into the river below, to make it look like a drowning accident. They did this simply because the girls were supposedly too Western. I am absolutely sure both parents chanted "Allah Akbar" ("Allah is great") right before they killed their daughters. Allah commanded Mohammed to kill anyone who is not a Muslim and who refuses to convert to Islam, sometimes in the most gruesome way possible. This is why Muslims doing beheadings always pray to Allah before they set the blade of their knife on a human neck to cut through the jugular veins, flesh, connective tissue, and bones. They chant, "Bisimillai Rahmoni Al Raheem," meaning, "I start killing this fellow human being in the name of Allah." This does not seem to be a merciful and beneficent god like Muslims and the Koran claim. There can never be a merciful way to behead a journalist, no beneficial way to rape someone, and no honourable way to abduct and take hostage an aid worker. Some Muslims will tell you that only the radical Muslims kill people, but this is simply a joke. The Koran clearly indicates that all Muslims must fight for the cause or support jihad and treat all non-Muslims as pagan. Allah and his followers have not been able to convince me that he is most merciful and most beneficent, for they failed to show a merciful way to kill, hate, and rape others.

Islam: A Religion of Peace or of Chaos and Death?

Religion can be described as a divine canopy of peace and tranquillity which shields the body and soul of believers away from the turbulence of the world. Religion is also seen as a model for decency and morality, where you can seek comfort in time of trouble, peace in time of sorrow, and succour when life's blows hit hard.

As discussed earlier in this book, we know that religion and faith have the ultimate power to control people's lives because these phenomena sit deep in the souls of their adherents and influence every facet of their existence. It affects their thoughts, attitudes, and behaviours, prescribing a dogmatic and zombie-like behaviour particular to that religion or faith group.

Based on the teachings of the idol, guru, Allah, or Jehovah – what- or whoever is the supreme controller of the faith – followers are spiritually obligated to follow the rules to the core. For example, a Rastafarian will be treated as an outcast if he abhors the dreadlocked hair and hates ganja, which they see as a spiritual connection with their root. A Sikh not covering his head will be a stranger in his kingdom; a Christian will look too strange going to church with a bottle of beer in one hand and a cigarette in the other, whereas a Muslim will not be welcomed into the Islamic world if he fails to fully comprehend the concept of jihad.

Among the determinants of human behaviour, which include environmental, parental, educational, and peer group influence, religion is the one that has the strongest influence. While you can easily reject or rebel against other developmental or behavioural factors, people find it difficult if not impossible to rebel against divine influence.

In my travels, I have been to many countries and seen many cultures in practice. I have seen many religions and faiths and their associated peculiarities. None of them preaches violence or embraces hate and violence like Islam does.

Buddhism, Sikhism, Rastafarianism, Christianity, and even paganism are not as hateful, sinful, or destructive as Islam. Others religions will not bother or persecute you for not being a member of their group. Islam, however, will not only hate you but also treat you as a pagan worthy of death. If a Muslim meets you for the first time, his or her first question will be "Are you Muslim?"' If you say no, that person will immediately treat you with disdain. We have not and will not hear of a Buddhist or Rastafarian that kills others for differing from his or her opinion, but Muslims will. While other religions use the power of persuasion, good examples, and perseverance to win followers, Islam uses force and submission to the will of Allah to bully, harass, intimidate, and kill you if you fail to submit. Mohammed killed more people in human history for not submitting to the will of his master than all devil worshippers in the world combined.

Atheists may rave and rant that there is no God until thy kingdom come; condemn the existence of Jesus Christ; and campaign for removal of crosses, nativity scenes, and religious aspects of Christmas until their last breaths. But they will never lift a finger to pinch your nose, not to mention talk about cutting off your head for not being an atheist. Even Satanists, known to engage in human sacrifice, would never have killed the millions of people killed by Islam.

There is a popular saying that whosoever is delighted in stepping on his or her own cloth will be more thrilled to shred another person's cloth. If Islam allows a woman and a man to bring a daughter into the world and then the parents jointly sentence her to death, bury part of her body, and cast the first stones to kill their daughter, then I think the whole world should stop being shocked when Islamic terrorism strikes like tornadoes on the streets. Rather, we should see them as who they are: a religion of chaos and death.

Most Islamic nations, including Saudi Arabia, Iran, Iraq, and Afghanistan are so shameless, heartless, and stupid that activists proudly show beheadings, instances of stoning, crucifixions, and other barbarity on YouTube videos or other websites as deterrents, but they end up exposing their backwardness and Satanism to the world. If you search for "beheadings or stoning in Iran, Afghanistan, Saudi Arabia, Somalia" on the Internet, you can see for yourself the horrors that will pop up on your screen. But let me warn you, you will see images that show you how horrible the kingdom of Satan in Islam can be.

It takes a sick mind to refer to a religion that skins human beings alive, cuts living people in two, removes babies from the uterus of a living pregnant woman, crucifies human beings alive, beheads living humans, and beheads people on mosque grounds, even babies, as a religion of peace.

Islam is so shamefully barbaric that most people who are unlucky enough to inherit the religion are appalled with what their faith is all about and are calling for a rewrite of the Sharia law and redesign of Islam, but the conservatives and the mullahs will never allow it.

Who Is the Antichrist?

Islam, Muslims, and the prophet Mohammed are the Antichrist. In 2 John: 22, we read, "Who is a liar but he that denies that Jesus is the Christ, He is an anti-Christ, that denies the Father and the Son." Most people have tried to avoid this revelation for centuries, simply because they cannot bring themselves to believe that their close friends, their family, or their neighbours are against the Messiah. Or maybe they don't admit it because Satan has deceived people for so long that he is also worthy of worship, merciful, and beneficent, whereas he is actually the great snake that deceived Adam and Eve at the beginning. He has diverted people's attention to other areas for so long that he now operates without suspicion; people think that the Antichrist means idol worshippers, Jews who denied the second coming of Christ or those who crucified him, or Adolf Hitler, the second-greatest killer after Islam. Some people are even waiting to see the Antichrist appear as a scary beast with multiple heads, one human eye, one eagle eye, one cow leg, and one elephant leg. But these ideas are all wrong. The passage quoted above tells us that the Antichrist is a liar who denies Jesus as the Christ.

These three characteristics are clearly found in Islam. In fact, Mohammed stated that God has no son, thereby denying the Holy Trinity of God the Father, God the Son, and God the Holy Spirit. No other religion has ever denied Jesus Christ as the Son of God; rather, they refrain from commenting on Him and run away at the mention of His name. Therefore, we can conclude that Islam is the Antichrist. This is why Islam kills hundreds of thousands of Christians across the world every year. They are out to gain the world for the prince Lucifer. May Jehovah deal with them according to their deeds.

Mohammed and his evil followers enjoy their conquest and domination of the world. For this to continue, he has brainwashed his followers to see Islam as a state and nation. They are not supposed to recognize any other power or authority on earth, whether of a monarch or government, outside of the Islamic enclave. Through his teachings, Mohammed removed the white and grey matter in his followers' brains and replaced it with cotton wool so their cerebral functions were permanently distorted. Muslims cannot think straight when shackled by Islam and its evil prophet. Allah has turned them into zombies who will do any foolish or ridiculous thing without giving it a thought. Why else would you agree to cut off your daughter's head or strap a bomb to yourself, knowing that it will send you to an agonizing and untimely death? Are you idiotic enough to believe the ridiculous promise that you will be rewarded with having sex with seventy virgins per day in heaven? No wonder Mohammed was able to leave the message with his evil believers that that Muslims across the globe are one brotherhood and one nation and that an attack on one of them is an attack on the others. They do not recognize any separation between Islam and state, so any conflict is easily and quickly interpreted as an attack on Muslims. The common outcry, "They are bombing our brothers, they are killing our children, and they are occupying our land," is always on the lips of Muslims sitting in a café in London or America, regarding battles between Afghanistan and Western coalition forces. However, they will never acknowledge that Osama bin Laden caused the conflict by commanding his men to leave their comfort zone in Afghanistan to knock down the Twin Towers and the Pentagon – among other targets – killing thousands of people on American soil and changing the face of international war. They will not tell you that Mullah Omar, the one-eyed Taliban leader of Afghanistan, was asked by the coalition led by President George W. Bush and Prime Minister Tony Blair to hand over Osama bin Laden to face justice, which would save his country from doom and destruction, but Omar chose the latter.

Muslims know from the bottom of their hearts that they are troublemakers and inciters of global conflicts, but they like committing acts of terror because these actions make the world dread them and governments scared of them. The master plan of Lucifer is to make the world bow to Islam, his chosen government and religion to compete with that of Jehovah. There has always been wartime and peacetime; unfortunately, this is the nature of the world. When non-Islamic nations go to war with other nations, they eventually find a resolution to the conflict. This is why the world has known relatively long periods of peace and quiescence, but the bastards in Islamic homes grew up and started to cause new waves of global conflicts that quickly turned into a perceived attack on their brothers and sisters. However, Muslims are hypocrites. Even in peacetime, they do not hesitate to hang their sisters or stone them to death for adultery, and they behead their brothers for treason if they bring shame on their clan by marrying someone from an unapproved clan. This is the barbarity of Islam. Unfortunately, some people who are uneducated, ignorant illiterates when it comes to Islamic affairs, such as Archbishop Desmond Tutu of South Africa, are not ashamed to carry a placard in protest with Muslims against the state of Israel. But what Desmond Tutu failed to realize is that while he was in a white collar and cassocks protesting with Muslims and jihadist, the only thing going through their minds was, "Look at this non-believer, a follower of Jesus – the bloody son of Mariam. Look at his aged neck. A day will come when we will slit his throat, bloody pagan."

If you are not convinced of their thinking, look at what the jihadists did to the British aid worker Alan Henning, a simple cab driver and kind-hearted husband and father who was moved to help by the plight of Syrian war-ravaged children. Alan was seen on videos, packing baby diapers and baby formula and cuddling Syrian infant – a friend in word and deed. In the same video, his Muslim "friends" in the background had heavy beards and scarves – one of which they gave to Alan Henning, and he proudly wrapped it around his neck. Lo and behold, Henning was later kidnapped by the same people he went to help. Despite all appeals to ISIS that Henning was a Good Samaritan who deserved to live, they chopped off his head and placed it on his back. So the next time Bishop Desmond Tutu goes out to do an ignorant humanitarian rally with his Muslim and Arab friends, he is advised to wear a metal collar beneath his bishop's collar. If the Muslims can slit the throat of Allan Henning, they will not hesitate to slit the throats of millions of others. No matter how good the intentions of these people are, Islam will always see them as pagans worthy of beheading. This is the nature of Islam and the ideology of your friends, so beware.

Why Are Criminals Easily Converted to Islam and Brainwashed?

In Europe and the United States, thousands of prison inmates have converted to Islam in the past decade. In fact, most jihadists, suicide bombers, and radical Islamic killers were criminals that converted to Islam while serving prison terms for rape, murder, kidnapping, burglary, money laundering, theft, and other social ills. When I hear about these conversions, I ask myself what the moral or spiritual motivations of these new converts was, and I wonder all the more at present, when there is no good associated with the religion but rather terrorism and barbarism. Later, as their activities provide a better understanding of the social and environmental biographies of these so-called converts, I was able to draw the conclusions that make up the remainder of this chapter.

The psychology of crime and behavioural genealogy of criminals has special affinity for Islam. This is because the mind of criminals and that of Islam have the same source of motivation: hate. A criminal must hate his or her victim and show no mercy before unleashing maximum terror. A criminal gains more from acting more hatefully. Islam, similarly, will not survive if there is no infidel to hate. Islam hates Jesus Christ and Christians because Jesus triumphed over Satan by dying on the cross at Calvary, bringing salvation to the world. Islam hates Jews because they are God's chosen people to whom the land of Canaan was given as an inheritance. Islam hates other religious people because it seeks to make them submit to its worship of the moon and star gods.

The evil forces of this world – the principalities and powers and Lucifer, their commander who operates inside every criminal –vowed allegiance to

Allah and promised to work for him, as mentioned in an earlier chapter. So, if a criminal inside a prison converts to Islam, it is simply a matter of joining a like group. In Mark 3: 23–26, Jesus says, "A house that divide against itself shall not stand and if Beelzebub the king of evil spirits divide against itself its kingdom will not stand." Evil spirits are able to identify themselves and bond together easily. This is why a murderer sitting in jail finds it rewarding to follow an imam who preaches jihad and human decapitation for the cause of Allah. They are conjoined at the hip by the spirits of hate and bloodthirstiness. I have no joy over the soul of an armed robber converting to Islam in prison, because he is just jumping out of the frying pan and into the fire, as the saying goes. The next time I see the same convert robbing banks to finance al-Qaeda, Hamas, Hezbollah, the Muslim brotherhood, Boko Haram or ISIS – all of which are groups vowed to the destruction of Jews, Christians, and humanity for the cause of Allah – I will simply say, "People of the same mind thinks alike."

In the Western countries formerly known as Christian nations, the concept of political correctness and so-called freedom has polluted the spiritual water of nations like Great Britain and the United States. They are abandoning the truth. Satan has sold false freedom and abandonment of the Christian faith to Great Britain, the United States, France, and other formerly Christian countries. For example, in England, the home of King James Bible, people only go to church three times in the course of their sojourn in this world: 1) at birth, during christening and baptism; 2) during marriage; and 3) during their funeral ceremony. Christian nomenclatures has been abandoned as primitive and cruel, and people can go to jail for preaching Jesus Christ on the street.

Because of this, the door of the West has been flung widely opened to every Tom, Dick, and Harry of the Islamic world. Mosques are freely erected in public spaces, but there has not and will not be a single church built in Saudi Arabia. However, Western governments never ask why this task seems like mission impossible. Satan, in his wickedness, pronounced through President Barrack Obama that America is no longer a Christian nation but a country of many nations in which Islam is growing like a wildfire. This is a trick of Lucifer to gain more ground in the heartland of Christianity and to attract more than enough followership to unleash its horror and terror at the appointed time. There's a saying that nature abhors a vacuum, and since the days of the Christian West are going away, people there now follow the lust of the flesh and grow deep in immorality. This provided the opportunity for Islam to brand the West as whores and as Satan. Islam then freely announces itself to the West as the only religion acceptable to God. Or imagine a child whose parent has never attended church or shown any religious leaning, not to mention Christian faith. If this young person sees a Muslim making noise about fasting for thirty days during Ramadan and saying that there is no God but Allah, such an unimpressionable child is most likely to fall to the public relations strategy of Islam, because he or she has only ever known a godless family.

Political correctness and overly pampering Muslim minorities in the West has gagged the political elite. In an attempt to secure votes, power, and oil money, politicians treated Muslims as sacred cows despite their lawlessness and lack of allegiance to the West. This gives Islam free reign to finance terrorism from the West and against the West, especially with Obama's satanic proclamation that America is not a Christian nation. The US government also gave approval for al-Qaeda to build a mosque on the site where the Twin Towers were knocked down, despite the fact that Christians in Muslim nations are being bombed daily. Therefore, Obama's declarations made the West an open recruitment ground for foreign jihadists. These warriors will soon take over and erect the flag of Sharia over the White House and Buckingham Palace if swift action is not taken by politicians in the West with common sense.

Islamic Concept of Salvation through Self-Destruction and Mass Killings

In the religious context, the term "salvation" means the redemption of one's soul and spiritual escape from earthly destruction to eternal comfort and safe haven in paradise. Salvation is a reward for dedication and obedience to the Supreme Being. In most cases, this comes at a price – for example, the sacrifice of precious blood for cleansing, atonement, and forgiveness of sins, leading to spiritual adoption.

To Christians, spiritual purification and adoption is achieved through Jesus Christ, who obeyed the will of God the Father by laying down his life for the sins of the world, so that whosoever shall believe in His name shall have eternal life (John 3: 15–16).

Ephesian 1: 3–7 describes our spiritual adoption as follows:

Blessed be the God and Father of our Lord Jesus Christ, who hath blessed us with all spiritual blessings in heavenly places in Christ. According as he hath chosen us in Him before the foundation of the world, that we should be holy and without blame before Him in love. Having predestined us unto the adoption of children by Jesus Christ to Himself, according to the good pleasure of His will. to the praise of the glory of His grace, wherein He hath made us accepted in the beloved. In whom we have redemption through His blood, the forgiveness of sins, according to the riches of His grace.

And Jesus Christ said in John 6: 53–56:

Verily, Verily, I say unto you, Except you eat the flesh of the Son of man, and drink His blood, ye have no life in you. Whoso eats my flesh, and drinks my blood, hath eternal life, and I will raise him up at the last day. For my flesh is meat indeed, and my blood is drink indeed. He that eats my flesh and drinks my blood, dwelt in me and me in him.

This is the concept of salvation as preached by the God of the Bible. Jesus and Father God did not ask people to kill themselves before inheriting his kingdom; they only need to believe in the name of the Lord and be saved. Anyone that kills him- or herself for the sake of salvation simply commits suicide and will go to hell.

Islam's concept of salvation is totally different, referred to as "*fida'e*". A suicide bomber is called a martyr or a sacrificial lamb to mimic the status of Jesus Christ, the sacrificial Lamb of God who took away the sins of the world as communicated in the Bible. A Palestinian woman whose son was killed while throwing rocks at an Israeli battalion proudly said, "My son died with a stone in his hand. I am proud of him; he is a martyr." The Koran teaches Muslims that the only way to enter paradise is to fight jihad and die as a martyr.

In Koran 3. 169, Allah gives assurance of salvation thus: "And never think of those who have been killed in the cause of Allah as dead, they are alive with their Lord, receiving provision. The pain that a martyr feels in death will be reduced so greatly that he will only feel as if he is being stung by a mosquito."

The Koran explains the six rewards for the homicidal perverts called an Islamic martyr as follows: 1) He will be forgiven with the first drop of his blood that is spilt. 2) He will see his place in paradise as he is dying. 3) He will be saved from the Great Horror on the day of judgement. 4) A crown of dignity will be placed on his head which contains many conundrums, each one being more precious than this life and all that it contains. 5) He will have seventy-two women (virgins of paradise), and 6) he will be allowed to intercede for seventy of his family members who would have otherwise gone to hell.

How could Jehovah give his majestic signature to this barbarity – shedding your own blood and that of innocent people in his own name? God is not a coward and a fool as Islam would like us to believe. If anyone errs against him, he has the power to either forgive the person or punish him or her in this world and in hellfire. He needs no middleman to fight his battle, as he controls all the legions of heaven and has the power to command what is visible and invisible. He is the Almighty God, who needs no suicide bomber to manage his kingdom in heaven and on earth.

Lucifer uses lies and tricks to sell this nonsense, trying to deceive people through Islam to expand his kingdom on earth and to lead many astray. Jesus Christ warned us this would happen, even among the elects. However, the fact remains that there is no other name under the sun through which man can be saved except Jesus Christ. God Almighty received his blood –not the blood of any murderer in the name of Islam – for salvation of mankind. Islamic martyrs, contrary to the false promises from the kingdom of Lucifer, will rot in hell, where there will be everlasting grief, sorrow, agony, pain, and gnashing of teeth if they fail to repent and accept Jesus Christ as their personal Lord and Saviour.

The bloodshed that Muslims commit echoes the blood that Cain, the first murderer in human history, shed when he killed his brother Abel. God turned Cain into a roaming beast with horns in his head so that no one would get close to him, thereby elongating his sorrow and shame. It was Abel whom God treated as a martyr and whose blood was so precious that it called for revenge. God told Cain, "The blood of your brother whom you shed has called unto me from the earth …" Satan entered into Cain, who had no previous knowledge of how to take human life, and he gave Cain a step-by-step guide of what to do. He continues murderous tutelage today by grooming and deceiving people to engage in jihad and beheadings, as demonstrated in Lucifer's hiring of the prophet Mohammed and his army. Like Cain, they will never be the true martyrs but rather satanic beasts and stateless fugitives, just like Cain, their ancestor and the first killer the world knew.

Christian Concept of Salvation through Shedding of Precious Blood of Jesus Christ

Much has been said about this topic, and a lot of biblical, scientific, and archaeological backing has been found to support the fact that our Lord and Saviour, Jesus Christ, was sent by God, born of the Virgin Mary, preached the gospel, and established the kingdom of his Father. He performed many miracles – healed the sick, opened blind eyes; opened deaf ears; healed the broken-hearted; called many to salvation; fed the hungry; opened barren wombs, rendered forgiveness of sins; healed paralytics; raised the dead; was envied by the high and mighty and feared by kings, powers, and principalities. Jesus was also persecuted by Satan, betrayed by Judas Iscariot, tried by the Roman emperor, and chastised by Roman guards. He carried his cross to Golgotha and was crucified in Calvary; even in the hour of death, he forgave the thief crucified on his right side. He asked his father, "Forgive them for they know not what they are doing." He gave up the ghost after saying, "It is finished."

Our Saviour was laid to rest in the tomb of Joseph of Arimathaea and was watched by Roman guards to prevent his disciples from sneaking him away and faking his promised resurrection. The guards attempted to stop the work of God Almighty, but on the third day, Jesus arose and showed himself to his disciples. People who had been deceased for a long time also rose from their graves, and people saw them on the streets heralding the almightiness of God. Therefore, the ploy of the Roman guards and elites to stop the news of salvation failed. Jesus has risen forever.

This is the record of salvation in Jesus Christ. He is without blemish or iniquity. Our Lord shed no human blood; rather, he shed his own blood for the redemption of all. There is a tower of mercy, not skulls; a river of redemption, not blood; and a free place guaranteed at the right hand of God, not hostages.

Jihadists and would-be suicide bombers, Jesus Christ died for your sins, and He will make you fishers of men. You were not created to be monsters; you were created in the image of God to love humanity, not hate them. Cutting off the heads of journalists and humanitarian workers and placing them on their backs is an act of Lucifer, not of Jehovah. God says in Psalm 18: 25, "With the merciful thou will show thyself as merciful." And in one of Jesus Christ's most popular sermons, the Beatitudes Jesus Christ said, "Blessed are the merciful: for they shall obtain mercy" (Matt. 5: 7). Hacking off the head of a humanitarian worker who comes to help provide comfort for your oppressed people is not an act of mercy, and it is definitely not a fight for God. If any religion promises you mercy in return for your barbarity, such as promising you seventy virgins in paradise, that religion is of the devil. But Jehovah God can still show mercy if you relinquish your evil ways and the barbaric religion that teaches people as young as five years old to decapitate their fellow humans. Follow Jesus Christ, whom Satan teaches you to hate, and become someone who fishes for men, not someone who beheads them.

The Christian and Islamic Views of Paradise Compared

Paradise—The Abode of God Almighty

To all who believe in God, in the power of his creation, and in his judgement at the end of time, paradise is a dream home. It is a place of comfort and everlasting joy, where God is the supreme ruler with no end. Christians believe that Jesus Christ will be the Prince of Peace, sitting at the right hand of the throne of Jehovah, from where he will judge the world.

Let us take a quick look at paradise as revealed by the Bible. Luke 16: 19–31 tells the following story of Lazarus and a rich man:

> There was a certain rich man, which was clothed in purple and fine linen, and fared sumptuously every day: And there was a certain beggar named Lazarus, which was laid at his gate, full of sores. And desiring to be fed with the crumbs which fell from the rich man's table: moreover the dogs came and licked his sores. And it came to pass, that the beggar died, and was carried by the angels into Abraham's bosom: the rich man also died, and was buried. And in hell he lift up his eyes, being in torments, and seeing Abraham afar off, and Lazarus in his bosom. And he cried and said, Father Abraham, have mercy on me, and send Lazarus that he may dip the tip of his finger in water, and cool my tongue; for I am tormented in flame. But Abraham said, son remember that thou in thy lifetime received thy good things, and likewise Lazarus evil things: but now he is comforted, and thou art tormented. And beside all this, between us and you there is a great gulf fixed: so that they which would pass from hence to you cannot: neither can

they pass to us that would come from thence. Then he said, I pray thee therefore, father, that thou will send him to my father's house:

For I have five brethren; that he may testify unto them, lest they also come into this place of torment. Abraham said unto him, they have Moses and the prophets; let them hear them. And he said, nay, father Abraham: but if one went unto them from the dead, they will repent. And he said unto him, if they hear not Moses and the prophets, neither will they be persuaded, though one rose from the dead.

In another part of the Bible, Jesus Christ gave us a glimpse into what happens in heaven. Matthew 22: 30 says, "For in the resurrection they neither marry, nor are given in marriage, but are as the angels of God in heaven."

These two descriptions came from Jesus Christ himself, who hailed from heaven and came into the world in human flesh. He gave us a few tips about his Father's kingdom.

1. Only people who are kind-hearted, meek, lovers of humanity who obey the Ten Commandments shall enter into paradise, the abode of God. Those who hate humankind and have blood on their hands will not.

2. All cruel people – the unkind, unjust members of society who behead their perceived enemies and perform other barbaric acts on earth – shall go to hell.

3. In heaven, there is no marriage, contrary to the Islamic story that seventy virgins shall be made available to jihadists.

Which version of paradise is more likely to be true? Should we believe Jesus Christ, who described the heavenly abode of God as a saintly place where only holiness is permitted, or Islam and Mohammed, who said paradise is where adultery and immorality exist? It doesn't take rocket science to know that the latter is not only false but satanically barbaric, for example, when the seventy virgins are promised as a reward for suicide bombers like those who blew up the Twin Towers.

If a greedy pig like the rich man in Lazarus' story was not given accommodation in paradise, there is no way a Muslim's penis will be constantly erect in God's city of holiness, not to mention that heaven is not a place for killers and murderers.

Holiness in Christianity and Islam Compared

Holiness can be described as a state of unrivalled sanctity, sainthood, and life without blemish which is eternally acceptable unto God. It is a life that mirrors the life of the heavenly angels and pleases God, our creator. Holiness radiates from the inner being outwards and portrays a godly life both in words and in deeds.

In Christianity, Jesus Christ enjoined His followers, "Be holy as your Lord God is holy." There is no blemish in God's kingdom. Our heavenly master also gave us the following instructions:

☐ Only those with clean hands and pure hearts shall ascend unto his holy mountain.

☐ Do not return evil for evil, but let your good shine for the world to see.

☐ Forgive us our sins as we forgive those who transgressed against us.

☐ If you are struck on the right cheek, turn unto them your left check, and if someone asks for your tunic, give that person your cloak also.

☐ Do unto others as you want them do unto you.

☐ If it is in your power, always be at peace with all men.

☐ If you are about to make your offering in front of the altar and you remember that you have a disagreement with your neighbour, leave the offering and first go to make amends with your enemy before you come back to your offering.

These are some of the holy attributes that Jesus Christ taught His followers

Jesus Christ personally lived these character traits. He would never hurt a fly, and he laid down his life for many. Holiness, in Christianity, does not place importance on outward appearances but on consecrating the inner mind. Jesus explained that whatever goes into the body does not make the body unholy but what comes out of the mind, such as adultery, idolatry, fornication, murder, hate, and shedding of innocent blood – as in beheading people or sentencing a pregnant woman to death for joining another religion. Worst still is the trend of killing humanitarians whose only crime is trying to help the needy.

Islam, on the other hand, believes holiness through rituals and outward appearances. It does not matter what you do – just wash your hands and your face five times daily. You can kill another person – just kill for Allah, and bow your head to kiss the ground in prayer with fresh human blood still on your hands.

In Islam, you must scrub your private part with water after urination; if there is no water around, you must wash it with sand or gravel. If you pray without performing these cleansing procedures, Allah will not answer your prayer. It is ridiculous to think that when praying in Islam and you accidentally pass flatulence, your prayer will not be answered. You have to go wash your bottom, hands, and face all over again before he would dare listen to you. The question now is, aren't the flatulence and urine part of the human body? What difference does it make whether they are inside or outside of it? If Allah can answer your prayer if they are concealed in your body, why can he hate you for bringing them out; does it mean that when they were inside you, they are actually not part of you? This is simply an act of hypocrisy to control Muslims. Jesus Christ said in Matthew 23: 26 and Luke 11: 39 that hypocrites wash the outside of their vessels, whilst the inside is full of dirt and germs. They like to wash their hands and possibly their faces and limbs before eating their bread, but their minds are full of evil and hate. This, I am sure, is a perfect reference to Islam if we look closely into their activities.

In Islam, holiness means lip service; you just need to be seen as cleansed to the visible eye, no matter what danger you pose to people around you. However, God cares less about how stinky your faeces or flatulence are than the tons of hate and destruction you unleash on the earth. If God can answer the prayers of people when they are trapped in a sewer and send others to their rescue, then your flatulence means nothing to Jehovah God when you call upon Him. Jehovah is different from Allah, and he is ready to hear your prayers with no strings attached.

Islam even permits parents to stone their children to death after returning from Friday prayers, whereas Jesus Christ told us of the forgiving father who threw a big feast for a prodigal son who squandered his inheritance. This is true love and holiness.

Covering yourself up from your face to your toes does not shield you from adultery, a disease of the mind. You will earn more respect from your creator when you are able to control your body from your mind by resisting adultery when your face is not covered and the temptation is higher. After all, there are some cases of men wearing a veil, disguising themselves as women to meet a woman in a veil to commit adultery. In such cases, in the Islamic world, the woman is stoned to death for not taking full control of her body, whereas the man who could not control his mind goes free. This is the height of hypocrisy.

My People Are Destroyed
for Lack of Knowledge

They say knowledge is power, and if this is true, then ignorance is weakness. In today's world full of evil, this type of weakness can be very dangerous and deadly.

Hosea 4: 6 warns, "My people are destroyed for lack of knowledge, I will also reject thee, that thou shall be no priest to me: seeing thou has forgotten the law of thy God, I will also forget thy children."

The preceding verse gives us insight into what is happening in the world today: the terrorism, the lack of a comprehensive understanding of Islam, and the wrong impression people have about Islam. After the events of 9/11, we woke up to what Islam and its beliefs actually mean.

For centuries, the lie that Islam was a religion of peace, a parallel religion to Christianity and Judaism, was successful. But with insiders and former terrorists openly teaching, preaching, and writing about Islam after decamping to Christianity with boldness and Jehovah's spiritual backing, we now have knowledge of what Islam really is.

The lack of knowledge about the evil in Islam – and sometimes the denial of the fact due to communal ties and political correctness – allowed the religion to grow so big in influence that it is very unlikely for the cancer of Islam to be completely surgically removed from the flesh of humanity.

Islam has been a clever and ever-evolving cancer, so that it has infected every nation on earth and is still growing unchecked. However, because ignorance leads to weakness, the world is now on the verge of collapse.

If urgent action is not taken to stop this evil ideology, Islam will act as the bomb of Armageddon to destroy the whole world. It will ultimately lead to the biblical prediction for the end of the world, a harbinger for the second coming of our Lord and Saviour, Jesus Christ, to gather the elect as he promised.

Islam has carried out a cancerous ravaging of the world before. The great Roman Empire, the most powerful nation on earth at that time, had a bitter taste of the affliction. Most Christian nations were destroyed and forced to convert to Islam. Millions of Christians, Jews, and others were killed until the jihadists were surgically removed by the coalition of Western powers in the name of the Crusaders. They challenged the evil Islamic army and defeated them everywhere they existed, removed the caliphate from existence and thereby saving the world. This is one prominent reason that every Islamic nation hates the Western nations unto this day.

Unfortunately, the world has developed permanent amnesia about the evil acts of Islam in the past. For the so-called humanitarian and politically correct reasons, they allowed the nations of Islam to become deeply rooted and powerful in the Western nations, thus bringing their caliphate right into the hearts of the Western nations. Once upon a time, when Muslims were terrorising and forcing the people of Uganda to embrace Islam and making all efforts to destroy the Christian and secular nature of Uganda – through violent jihad and intimidation – President Idi Amin was very quick to deal with their threats and send them packing from his country. Both young and old were thrown out, en masse, and secular peace was restored in Uganda. However, Great Britain saw this as a cruel act, so they gave the Islamists automatic asylum in Britain, allowing for the spread of jihad in Britain and the foundation for Islamic fundamentalisms in Europe to this day. Therefore, it's no wonder that the Islamic presence in the United Kingdom boasts about erecting the flag of Islam on top of Westminster and Buckingham Palace soon. Considering the rate at which people from the Islamic nations are giving birth and multiplying in Great Britain today, it could actually happen.

As aforementioned, President Barack Obama has stated that the United States is a country made up of many nations. A hundred-year-old damaged church near the bombed World Trade Centre was not given a permit or assistance to rebuild, but Obama – who has Islamic blood running in his veins – announced that an Islamic centre called "Kodorba", meaning "victory against enemy" in Arabic will be built on a site near the former Twin Towers. While Americans argue that the jihadists should not be allowed to do this, Obama simply replied, "Muslims have got the right to build their mosque near the knocked down WTC, period." With his ignorance and lack of knowledge, Obama handed America – once a Christian nation – to Islam.

Prime Minister David Cameron went on air to talk tough about the barbarity of the ISIS, but he ended by saying, "The barbarity of ISIS does not represent Islam, as Muslims are peace-loving and Islam is a religion of peace." But he failed to mention that all terrorists who have existed so far have been Muslims. Because of political correctness, he also failed to acknowledge that Britain has produced violent terrorists like Omar Bokri, Anjem Choudry, and Abu Hamza – the hook-handed Osama bin Laden of the West – and other Islamic killers who established a Sharia-ruled zone in the heart of London. Stoning, flogging, beheading and honour killings regularly take place in the UK.

The lack of knowledge about the evil that Islam represents made the West allow their streets and homes to be flooded by thousands of Islamic women who give birth daily at the expense of British taxpayers. Unfortunately, these children will soon grow up as mujahideen and do nothing short of beheading British citizens who refuse to bow down to Islam and forcing others to become slaves of Allah.

Due to a lack of knowledge, the leaders of France allowed their country to be overpopulated by Muslims, only to wake up one day and find their streets and motorways obstructed every Friday by hypocritical Muslims knocking their heads on tarmacs meant for busses and commuters. France, the United Kingdom, the United States, Germany, and other Western nations asked for cheap labour from the Arabian deserts and they got cheap death on top. They wanted loyal Muslims who could be spoiled with fast food, chocolate, and cups of tea into deserting their hostile religion. Alas, they instead suffered attacks, beheaded soldiers on the street, and a mass shooting from Nadal Hassan, who yelled, "Allah Akbar," before turning the gun on his fellow soldiers and killed dozens of them.

Out of their lack of knowledge, the West allowed mosques to litter their nations, whereas no building permit will ever be given to a church in Saudi Arabia. Old churches predating Islam are being destroyed in the Arab lands. Christian faithful are being killed and chased out of their ancestral lands. The only "benefit" the West gets from this unholy alliance is the lofts and basements of mosques in their land being filled to the brim with bullets, guns, grenades, and bomb-making equipment to kill and maim their host nations.

Due to their lack of knowledge, the West was quick to give citizenship to Muslims, hoping that it would remove the hair of homeland affinity from their heads. In return, the West saw a massive exodus of naturalized jihadists return to their mother lands of Syria, Iran, Iraq, Afghanistan, and Pakistan to behead Westerners and launch terror into Western nations from abroad. Worst still, they revered their hostile leaders, imams, and sheiks and called for death to the Western leaders. They pledged to fly the flags of Sharia over the White House, Westminster, Buckingham Palace, and all over the West. If the ignorance and weakness of the West continues, their dream of Islam taking over will be comfortably achieved in the next fifty years.

Western leaders, because of a lack of knowledge, deviated from the fight that their ancestors took to the jihadists, the Crusades, centuries ago. This conflict led to the defeat of Islam and the death and terror it unleashed on the world at the time, which is why Islam hates the West today and will do anything to destroy it.

Due to a lack of knowledge that will predispose and precipitate the destruction of Western nations and Christianity, the British, French, Americans, German, and other Western governments fail to realize that rapid empowerment of Muslims through social entitlements. Things such as free food, free housing, free health care, free giro, free halal food in hospital, and free interpreter services cost billions of pounds and dollars yearly, and they provide comforts and breeding grounds for Muslims to freely do business and give birth to multiply their population rapidly.

More ignorantly, the West always allows themselves to be fooled into thinking that poverty and a lack of educational and medical facilities, coupled with a lack of social facilities and empowerment, are the reasons

Muslims turns to terrorism. They believe that if they pump more money into the Middle East and pamper their citizenry with more goodies, Muslims will denounce terrorism. But this is pure nonsense that comes from misunderstanding Islam. If these are the reasons for the war Islam is waging on the world, why do educated and professional people become suicide bombers and foreign jihadists?. A medical doctor was among the bombers who rammed their cars full of explosives into the Glasgow airport many years ago. Jihadi John, Richard, and Abdulmutalab were not illiterates. Similarly, illiterates and poor people did not fly the aeroplanes into the Twin Towers. Nada Rafal is a military psychiatrist. So, what nonsense are you talking about? Muslims are richer than those in the west. A single emir In the Middle East can pay the salary of everyone in the queen's household, and yet he finances terrorism because that is his religious obligation. They don't care if the unrest in their land makes them poorer. They must force nonbelievers to bow to the sword of Islam.

Fifty-Year Prediction of Doom

In the next fifty years, all Western nations and especially Great Britain will be overrun and governed by the Islamists. A Sharia flag will fly on top of Westminster, the White House, Buckingham Palace, and others. The triggers that will make this happen are as follows:

1. White people are drastically cutting back on the number of children they bear, and some of them prefer to have no children at all, thus drastically reducing the number of people with Western ancestry. The trick of Satan is to reduce this population to far below fighting level. Gays and lesbians tend not to bear many children either. Even heterosexual parents simply prefer having only one child. If this pattern continues, few white people will be roaming the Western nations in the next fifty years.

2. Muslim families in the West, however, have turned themselves into baby-making factories. Despite government clampdowns on families from other religious backgrounds to marry just one wife in compliance with the monogamous mentality of the West, Muslim men are allowed to marry more than one wife in acceptance of their polygamist tradition. This allows Muslim men to procreate easily, thus deliberately producing more kids than they could have

dreamt of in their poverty-stricken nations. Who wouldn't, with free health care and childbirth services? The more children you have, the more housing benefits you get. And if you do go from an illiterate and poverty-stricken nation to being rewarded just for opening your lap and producing babies like termites, it is no surprise the sky would be your limit.

3. There is one rule for Muslims, and another rule for the rest. England treats Muslims as an endangered species. Those from other backgrounds must learn English and blend in with society to benefit from societal provisions, whereas Muslims can live in Great Britain for two decades without learning to read and write. They can cover their face from head to toe in isolating veils and shout, "Death to the Queen," without any consequence. Muslims can pray in the workplace five times a day, cutting down on their work hours and wasting revenue. However, a Christian cannot mention prayer or talk about Jesus Christ. If they do, the wrath of the Christ-less West will be unchained immediately. A British Airways staff lost her job simply for wearing a necklace with a cross. What a shame it is to see a Christian nation turn into the devil's enclave.

4. Majority carries the vote. Because Islam was a political estate before its transformation into a religion, the thing that Muslims does best is politics. They know which candidate to throw their weight behind, even on foreign soil, and they are very good in using their mosque pulpits as campaign mouthpieces. This is why, after 9/11, American Muslims quickly abandoned President George W. Bush for waging war on their sheikh, Osama bin Laden, and al-Qaida. They also threw their weight behind Barack Obama as one of their own, and it seems they made the right choice; the freedom Islam has enjoyed under Obama is unrivalled. In Britain, Tony Blair was dumped by Muslims, and George Galloway became the new Muslim ruler of the West and the Islamic ambassador for Iran in the United Kingdom for his support of the Islamic agenda against the West and Israel. As long as there are Muslim votes in his constituency, no candidate can defeat Galloway.

In the next fifty years, the Muslim population in the West will have grown large enough to consume both indigenous and foreign residents. Therefore, the number of mujahideen will outnumber the male population of European ancestry in the West.

5. Islam's goal and purpose: The desire of Muslims has always been to conquer the West for being the only major power that can stop them from advancing brutal cause of Islam. They are ready for battle and anxious to penetrate deep into the fabric of the West to hit them where it matters. The Bible gave a hint regarding Ishmael, saying that "when he grows old, he shall remove the bondage from himself." Muslims want to keep their heads down until they become too strong and powerful for the Western nations to resist their wrath. Then they will unleash the terror of Allah on the West as they did to other nations they have conquered.

6. Defeated in sleep:- By the time that the mujahideen living in the West put to use their brutal jihadi skills to bear on every non-believer of Islam, it will be too late for the party-loving and beer-drinking western young males and the politicians, whose sense of patriotism and sense of protecting state and religion will have been eroded by political correctness and dummy laws and regulations, will crumble under the weapons – perhaps even a nuclear bomb – of Allah from Iran and ISIS. They will be defeated in their sleep, as forewarned by Jesus Christ that "during sleep the enemy came and sowed weeds in the field."

7. Too late to recover if not stopped: If the Islamist power in the West is not stopped in its formative stage, it will be unstoppable, with devastating consequences. Muslim or not, we will all be doomed by the aftermath of global inaction. I belief that most Muslims ignorantly practice their religion with genuine belief that it is from God, only to discover that it is not what they bargained for. Because of their familiarity with and social connection to the faith, they find it difficult if not impossible to quit. However, if going to paradise is worth working for, it is never too late for them to consider their stance and convert to Christianity, as Jesus Christ is the only way to heaven. Even the prophet Mohammed, after realizing his wrong choice with Islam, lamented, "It is sensible

to follow he who knows the way," in reference to Jesus Christ. Imagine ISIS having a nuclear weapon and writing "Allah Akbar" on it to destroy the non-believers. It would be a falling sky which affects everyone.

8. Nip the beast in the bud. The governments of the West should use common sense and political jurisprudence to tame the beast of Islam before it kills everyone there. How many years did it take the United Kingdom to deport terrorist Abu Qatada to Jordan, his homeland, where he was wanted for terrorizing his motherland? How many millions in taxpayer money were wasted in nurturing Abu Hamza and his evil family that gave nothing back to the United Kingdom, apart from radicalizing young Muslims to bomb the UK and her allies. Anjem Choudary trained to become a lawyer with UK taxpayer money, and he gave nothing back to his beneficiary nation, apart from taking over where Abu Hamza, his mentor in crimes against humanity, left the reins of terror before his extradition to a US jail. Anjem Choudary was arrested in September 2014 in connection with sponsoring terrorism and spewing hatred, by building a Sharia zone in the United Kingdom, where he openly terrorized non-Muslims. Too much money has been spent building his Islamic empire in London and abroad. This stupidity must stop if humanity is to be saved from the cancer of Islam.

I have several suggestions for how to prevent the predicted doom.

1. Let any Middle Eastern or Islamic jihadists caught in the act be stripped of their citizenship, along their family members, and immediately deported to their motherland, where they belong. If Idi Amin could do it successfully, why can't you do it to save your land? There are other problems facing Uganda today, but thanks to Idi Amin, Islamic terrorism is not one of them.

2. Ban the evil curtain that separates Islamic women from the world – the veil or hijab. After all, it has been used to disguise wanted terrorists who ran away from the reach of justice. Do not wait until bombs and explosives are carried into the heart of a supermarket by a suicide bomber. If such weapons can be hidden inside a

turban with deadly impact to kill an ex-president in Pakistan, a burka in the heart of an American supermarket could conceal a more destructive explosive device. Please ban its use in the West.

3. Go back to church. Christianity is shrinking in the West and completely disappeared in the Middle East, whereas Islam dominates the Middle East and is growing rapidly in the West. To stop it, go back to church; your ancestors published the King James Bible and sent missionaries to Africa, Asia, and other parts of the globe. Jesus is love. Don't replace him with Allah, whose mission is to destroy you. Do not give Satan the chance.

4. Shut down any mosque that teaches kids how to carry out beheadings of infidels any mosque that is used as a depot for bomb-making equipment and ammunitions must be sealed up forever, and if necessary, every mosque in the West must be closed down. After all, they are built to spread hate and jihadism.

5. If Christians and other non-Muslims continue to be butchered in Islamic nations and permission is not given to build churches in Saudi Arabia, Muslims in the West must be sent back to their desert gulags. Christians facing persecution in Muslim nations must also be brought to the safety of the West.

6. All Western citizens that travel overseas to wage war against the West must be automatically stripped of their citizenship and barred from coming back to the United Kingdom. If they dare return, they must be arrested as traitors.

7. Bring back the death penalty. Muslims like Adebowale, Adebolajos, and Abdumuttalabs must be given the death sentence. People who show no mercy deserves no mercy, period.

Do you ever wonder why there is so much unbearable chaos in the world under the reign of President Obama in America, while al-Qaeda rapidly transformed into more dangerous groups like Boko Haram and ISIS under his nose? Many Islamic threats, including the Boston Marathon bombing, beheadings in Oklahoma, and the Nadal massacre took place under President Obama's nose. The reason is simple: he lacks knowledge of Islam. He is simply a bystander who saw people carrying the Koran and going to mosque and concluded that he was an authority in Islam, but he got it completely wrong.

President Obama is simply a traitor, a pagan, and a deserter who has a fatwa on his head for even though he was born a Muslim, he converted to Christianity. Whether his profession of Christianity is genuine or fake is a question for another time.

Because of his lack of knowledge, Obama declared the Muslim Brotherhood in Egypt a modern and moderate Islamic and humanitarian organization, and he ferried its leader to presidency by throwing Hosni Mubarak under the bus. This happened despite warnings from sensible and America-loving leaders to help peace reign in the region. Only when President Mohammed Mossi started to order the execution of Christians and other people not in line with his group's radical view of Islam did Obama realize his folly.

A group called the state of Islam is a powerful backer of Barack Obama; in the past, Obama has praised a terrorist leader Abdallah bin Bayyah, who called for the beheading of American soldiers around the world as a moderate Muslim. I would not be surprised if President Obama calls the Boko Haram saints and angels by the time he leaves office. He has allowed Islamic terrorism to flourish globally due to his lack of knowledge. His weakness out of ignorance has thus made the world a more dangerous place for us all.

Obama always boasts of killing Osama bin Laden and putting al-Qaeda on the run. But the fact is, the hunt for Osama bin Laden was almost ten years in the making, started by President George W. Bush who put a formidable team of soldiers in place and gave them every tool needed to track down and kill or capture Bin Laden, and this master plan simply came to fruition under the watch of Barack Obama. What happened to the Pakistani doctor who helped America pinpoint where bin Laden lives and confirmed his identity? He is now serving a life sentence in Pakistani prison as punishment for selling out his father's religion. Any sensible leader would have extracted this man from Pakistan before the raid took place. Why is Obama dying to close the Guantanamo Bay detention camp, and why is he so friendly with Iran, employing every trick in his books to make sure Iran obtains a nuclear weapon – which we know will become one of the Armageddon weapons one day. Why is Obama so hateful of Israel and spiteful of its prime minister, Netanyahu? Furthermore, why has Obama never referred to the Islamic war of terror on the world as an act of terror but as workplace turbulence? Why did Obama proudly swap six dangerous Taliban fighters for one deserting Muslim American soldier?

This is an act of Lucifer to use people in high places to fight his war against Christ. In my opinion, just like he found a perfect hireling in Mohammed in the past, Satan found one in President Obama. His Islamic ancestry and romance with extreme left-wing radicals of the world combined to make him an ideal prospect.

If anyone remains under the illusion that Islam is a religion of peace that must be given undeterred liberty, that person should wait until more beheadings take place in his or her midst. Remember, only devil worshippers do beheadings and human rituals, and Islam is not an exemption, no matter how bitter the truth sounds. After all, demons have vowed to worship the God of the Koran and pay allegiance to Allah. Hence, any beheadings carried out by evil people are simply a fulfilment of these agreements.

Love for God Hate for God Concept;- I was shocked to my bone marrows during a conversation with a Muslim who proudly, religiously and arrogantly told me, ''I love for God and I hate for God'' This is the mentality that push Muslims to commit horrible crimes against humanity in the name of their religion and love for Allah.

We have seen a British soldier beheaded on a busy street of London in broad daylight. A few months later, a British woman was beheaded in another London street. And a few months after that took place, an Oklahoma convert to Muslim, Alton Nolen, beheaded an American woman because people refused to convert to Islam. Nadal previously killed his fellow soldiers without provocation. All of these people shouted "Allah Akbar" before chopping off the heads of their victims. If the West calls Islam a friend, they should continue to nurture them and let them multiply. In the next fifty years, they will see the truth when the swords of Islam chop off human heads like banana trees on the streets.

The Perilous Time

Second Timothy 3: 1 says, "This know also, that in the last days perilous times shall come. For men shall be lovers of their own selves, covetous, boasters, proud, blasphemers, disobedient to parents, unthankful, unholy."

We established previously that the only way to recognize the only prophet of Jehovah is by determining whose prediction comes true. So far, this prophet has consistently been Jesus Christ, as we shall see below.

Matthew 24: 5, Mark 13: 6, and Luke 21: 8 – Many will come in the name of Jesus Christ and deceive many. Imagine Jesus Christ seeing so-called men of God robbing and duping their congregations today from over 2,000 years ago.

Matthew 24: 7–8, Luke 21: 11, Mark 13: 8 – The first sign of sorrow comes in calamities, famines, pestilences, earthquakes in diverse places, fearful sights, and great signs in heaven. Imagine predicting famine in the days when food was grown in abundance.

Matthew 24: 9, Luke 21: 12–15, Mark 13: 9–11 – Christians will be hated, delivered up, killed, and persecuted by all nations.

Matthew 24: 6–7, Luke 21: 9–10, Mark 13: 7–8 – There will be wars and rumours of war between nations and kingdoms. Look at the world today, and see this prophecy of our Messiah coming true.

Matthew 24: 10, Mark 13: 12–13, Luke 21: 16–17 – Men will hate and betray each other everywhere.

Matthew 24: 11 – Many false prophets will appear and deceive many. There's nothing better to justify the prophecy of our Lord Jesus Christ than the activities of so-called men of God today; church money is diverted to the pastors' use. They collect tithes, offerings, and pastoral gifts, ignoring the saying of Jesus Christ that "you shall forever have poor people among you." Instead of spending God's money on the poor among us, they boast that they are on the world's rich list. Some of them even own two or three private jets, while poor people die of starvation around them. The situation is worse in Africa, where "men of God" arrange fake miracle and steal new-born babies from their parents in delivery wards to sell as "miracle babies". What a shame.

The list of confirmed predictions of Jesus Christ is endless, as laid out by Father Seraphim Rose of the Catholic Church and many others.

In Matthew 24: 15–22, Jesus Christ warned us of the calamities we witness today.

> When you therefore shall see the abomination of desolation, spoken of by Daniel the prophet, stand in the holy place, (Whoso reads, let him understand:) Then let them which be in Judea flee into the mountains. Let him which is on the housetop not come down to take anything out of his house. Neither let him which is in the field return back to take his clothes. And woe unto them that are with child, and to them that give suck in those days! But pray that your flight be not in the winter, neither on the Sabbath day. For then shall be great tribulation, such as was not since the beginning of the world to this time, no, nor ever shall be.

From the time I was a child reading the Bible until the 9/11 attacks, I always wondered what that desolation, abomination, and tribulation meant and what it would look like. But seeing jumbo jets full of human beings hijacked by evil men and deliberately used as missiles to kill themselves and innocent people, I was immediately reminded of this Bible passage. The particular statement that kept flashing repeatedly in my mind was Matthew 24: 21, which says, "For there shall be great tribulation, such as was not since the beginning of the world to this time." Ever since then, I am more convinced than ever that Jesus Christ was prophesying about the threat from those who eternally vowed to destroy his father's kingdom – Lucifer and his hirelings, also known as the followers of the prophet Mohammed.

In Matthew 24: 22, Jesus Christ warns that unless the world acts fast, we shall all be doomed as follows: "Except those days should be shortened, there should no flesh be saved: but for the elect's sake those days shall be shortened."

While preparing Christians for the persecutions we would face from the Antichrist, Jesus Christ warned us about the identity of the enemy the world would face when describing Satan and his collaborators and hirelings. "You are of your father the devil, and the lust of your father ye will do. He was a murderer from the beginning, and abode not in the truth, because there is no truth in him. When he speaks a lie, he speaks of his own; for he is a liar, and the father of it" (John 8: 44).

The Bomb of Armageddon

Naïve or willingly ignorant people and politicians that suffers from deliberate amnesia brand some Muslims as moderates and some as terrorists, but history has revealed that the prophet Mohammed led the first caliphate, wherein he killed over one and a half million Armenians. This is not a hypothesis but fact.

Armageddon is a destruction of apocalyptic proportions, where nothing will be spared, animate or inanimate. It will operate like thousands of falling meteors that leave thousands of meters' worth of craters in depth and circumference in which every structure within the touch of its impact shall be pulverised into thin air. It will contain rage and fury a trillion times more turbulent than all the volcanic eruptions and tsunamis of the world combined.

What is going to aggravate this Armageddon? There will be a battle between darkness and light, God and Satan, good and evil. It will be a battle for dominion by principalities and powers, with the aim of expanding their satanic empire and eliminating the kingdom of Jehovah on earth.

God felt so sorry for the earth when the great beast, Lucifer, entered it in anticipation of the chaos and confusion he would bring to humanity 1 Timothy 4: 1–3 says, "Now the spirit speaks expressly, that in the later times some shall depart from the faith, giving heed to seducing spirits, and doctrines of devils. Speaking lies in hypocrisy; having their conscience seared with a hot iron; Forbidding to marry, and commanding to abstain from meat, which God has created to be received with thanksgiving of them which believe and know the truth."

It's little wonder that Greenpeace campaigners, abortionists, gay and lesbian advocates, and atheists are more comfortable with Islam than Christianity.

In 2 Timothy 4: 3–4, the Bible warns, "For the time will come when they will not endure sound doctrine; but after their own lusts shall they heap to themselves teachers, having itching ears. And they shall turn away their ears from the truth, and shall be turned unto fables."

Lucifer's goal is to make this world his own kingdom; he left heaven after the great rebellion to come to the world so that he could get a place to rule and establish his kingdom, so why would God share his kingdom with him? Satan is ready to fight to the death to make sure he wins this world, and he will not hesitate to lie and deceive along the way.

Lucifer's tool of recruitment is the lust of the flesh, and as people in the West say, "Do whatever makes you happy." This contradicts the warning from God that not all that is profitable is good for the sustenance of human soul. Because people are vulnerable to acts of the flesh, Lucifer will always dangle this dangerous carrot in front of them. He tempts us in the form of adultery, idolatry, lies, stealing, rape, armed robbery, fraud, kidnapping, gambling, dishonesty, covetousness, divorce, Satanism, lesbianism, gayness, alcoholism, murder, abandoning the faith, and so on.

Because Lucifer's spirit is the common denominator, lustful people always team up to advance the kingdom of Satan and deplete the kingdom of Jehovah. Fewer people go to church, and even among the churchgoers, sound doctrine is very hard to come by. Most pastors are worshippers of their belly rather than followers of God. Fights within a church and between churches are the order of the day for the sake of money, position, and wealth. This leads to churches breaking up and setting up simply for economic purposes. Gone are the days of "many are called but few are chosen"; today, fewer are called, but many are recruited. Whenever joblessness or greed pops up, the main recruitment centre is the church and the pastoral business. The body of Christ is sending more candidates to the kingdom of Lucifer through the actions of so-called men and women of God. Similarly, if a police officer is caught in the act of stealing, one can imagine that armed robbery will surely become the order of the day in that city.

But our Lord has predicted that all people shall become lustful and worshippers of their belly more than worshipping him, and many shall stray and abandon the faith. However, we have been warned, "Let those that stand beware, lest they fall."

But making people fall is the job that Lucifer knows best, because those who part ways with Jehovah God can become the devil's hirelings and worshippers. Their common pursuit is to destroy Christianity, Judaism, and the kingdom of God. This evil collaboration brings the enemies of Christ together to preach immoralities and discourage others from following Jesus Christ.

The enmity and hatred that will be unleashed on Christianity was first predicted by a holy man named Simeon, who awaited the coming of the Messiah his whole life. When Jesus Christ's parents brought him to the temple to be blessed after his birth, Simeon made this ever-relevant prediction: "And Simeon blessed them, and said unto Mary his mother, Behold, this child is set for the fall and rising again of many in Israel; and for a sign which shall be spoken against" (Luke 2: 34). The last line is noteworthy: Jesus Christ and his signs and church shall be spoken against by Lucifer and his followers.

Now, with the followers of Satan multiplying like bacteria, what weapon are they going to use to bring about Armageddon? Islamists and their Antichrist allies have used hate, imprisonment, floggings, beheadings, mass killings, genocide, crucifixion, suicide bombings, pant bombings, shoe bombings, cargo bombings, bicycle bombings, aeroplane bombings, turban bombings, and many tactics to cause terror and intimidation. They hope to force people to submit to the will of Allah and the lordship of their prophet Mohammed, but as Jesus Christ promised his followers, the kingdom of His Father has been established. The power of Satan shall not prevail over it; Christianity continues to take pre-eminence in the world as the only religion that can guarantee eternity in paradise.

But the fury of Satan is about to break lose. The Islamic Republic of Iran is in the forefront of nations fighting fiercely to acquire nuclear weapons, and a game changer is about to be seen in the battle between the armies of God and of Lucifer. This reminds me of wise saying that states, "An enemy that willingly knocks you on the ground is not far away from killing you if he so desires." In other words, a Jihadi John that beheads people giving out bread and water to starving people in refugee camps with a butcher's knife will find it easy to annihilate the entire human race if he manages to lay his hands on a nuclear weapon.

Imagine if ISIS teams up with the Islamic State of Iran in possession of nuclear weapons, both with a burning zeal to welcome the arrival of "Imam Mahdi", which they claim is coming to bring every nation on earth to bow to the evil caliphate of Islam by force, and no one will be spared. If you thought the number of Armenians Mohammed killed was devastating, then wait until ISIL and Iran and their satanic allies inscribe "Allah Akbar" on hundreds of nuclear warheads and fire them into nations of pagans that refuse to bow to the will of Allah. You are looking at a disaster the size of hundreds of thousands of Hiroshima and Nagasaki bombings combined, and the Muslims will have no mercy. The Koran commands, "Oh ye that believes, show no mercies on the non-believers, the kefirs, behead them with the edge of your swords."

Any government that allows an Islamic nation to possess nuclear weapons is nothing but ignorant, naïve, and an enemy of humanity. Such leaders are hirelings of Lucifer, collaborating to fight the kingdom of Jehovah God.

For about ten years, the former Iran president begged Allah during every United Nations meeting to help him hasten the return of the Mardi, the Islamic version of the second coming of Jesus Christ. The Iranian ayatollahs and every Muslim on earth are trained to believe that Mohammed will come back and rule the world in a caliphate that will be the only government on earth, and it is the duty of every living Muslim to make this happen. The primary aim of Osama bin Laden was to destroy the United States, dubbed the Great Satan. His mentality was to stop Saudi Arabia from having anything to do with the United States. It's no wonder that people in Iran, Iraq, Pakistan, Sudan, and most Islamic countries, including northern Nigeria, were on the streets, celebrating the fall of the Twin Towers. Almost 4,000 multinationals were killed, all yelling the satanic chant, "Allah Akbar". They shall yell it again if Obama allows Iran to possess nuclear weapons, as I am sure he will.

Obama is so soft on Iran, and he sends secret letters to the ayatollahs of Tehran to hasten dialogue on the acquisition of nuclear technology, whereas he is very hostile toward Israel. If negotiations succeed, Iran will surely hasten the arrival of Imam Mardi by wiping Israel and Bethlehem off the face of the earth, and Barack Obama will be unofficially announced as the greatest Satan of our time. However, I am sure this is not a legacy that Obama would like to leave. Iran believes that Mohammed will reappear from a certain well in the desert of Iran, from where he will form a caliphate to rule the world by Sharia law. The Iranians are so fanatically silly about this ideology that president Ahmadinejad has built a gigantic and opulent mosque to house this well from which his messiah will appear. He has also constructed an underground railway to transport believers to and from the mosque that will be the caliphate. This is evidence that Islamists about wanting everyone to convert or be killed.

River Jordan in the same present day Jordan ruled by king Abdallah is the river in which the Messiah of the world, Jesus Christ was baptised showing the footprint of Christianity in the region, centuries before the birth of prophet Mohammed and formation of Islam. But today, Christians no more own the land because their have been systematic genocide of Christians in the region by dominating forces of Islam.

Damascus, in Syria, was once a Christian city, thousands of years before the birth of Mohammed. Matthew 4: 24 tells us, "And his [Jesus's] fame went throughout all Syria; and they brought unto him all sick people that were taken with divers diseases and torments, and those which were lunatic, and those which had the palsy; and he healed them." Have you ever wondered why this place where Christ Jesus performed miracles in the name of his Father could now be handed over by that same God to ISIS and the jihadists, whose only "miracle" is to hack off people's heads.

The answer is that Jehovah is not the same as Allah, and Jehovah did not abandon Jesus to embrace Muslim warriors. Rather, Lucifer fell from heaven, came to the world, and hired them to advance his cause. If drastic action is not taken, then the West and then the whole world will soon become the territory of the Imam Mahdi – the mysterious man who in the opinion of the mullahs and jihadists will reappears from his well and enthrones his evil caliphate.

The bomb of Armageddon is on a fast track to the production line. ISIS, Hezbollah, the Muslim Brotherhood, Iran, Hamas, Jihadi John, lone wolves, hatchet attackers, –those who behead non-Muslims, and other Islamic horrors yet to show their identity pose a serious threat to the world.

In the past, these forces haven't had strong backing from elsewhere, but now – knowingly or unknowingly – the current world leadership under Barrack Obama has created an unprecedented atmosphere conducive for jihadists. He makes relentless efforts to close the detention facility at Guantanamo Bay, and because the trials of Islamic mass murderers are taking place in the civil court instead of military courts, they are less likely to be treated as enemy combatants and given the death sentence they deserve and pray for. The more of these idiots we send into premature martyrdom, the better it is for the world, as they do not belong to the human community but to an assembly of evil men burning day and night in hell. The Obama administration has downplayed Christ and the cross; Christians are being killed by the thousands worldwide, and President Obama utters no word of condemnation about it. He removed the strong military presence capable of ruling the Middle East and maintaining peace and replaced them with weaklings who allow terrorism to thrive and allow ISIS to be formed. He replaced the soldiers protecting democracy with the Iranians and ISIL. Worst still, illegal aliens are now free to enlist in the US Army without any background checks. Who cares if ISIL, jihadists, and other haters of Israel and America gain free access to the world's most powerful weapons and turns them against Christian nations to achieve their long-awaited Armageddon? The world needs a lot of prayer to stop these evil collaborators from rapidly gaining momentum. President George W. Bush recognized the danger of Iraq gaining nuclear weapons capability and was quick to disrupt the programme, but President Obama apparently has no problem with Iran acquiring ballistic missiles. He is spending enough time in office for the ayatollahs in Tehran to buy and make an Armageddon-scale bomb, not minding the deadly consequences to Israel, America, and other Western Civilization.

Voices speaking against the rise of Islam in the west are being squashed. A good example is Mr Geert Wilders, the parliamentary leader for the Party for Freedom in the Netherlands. He has always been tagged as anti-Islam and through visa bans is constantly prevented from freely travelling across Europe, for fear of upsetting Muslims, failing to realise that if the west fail to upset Muslims, Muslims will surely upset them. Meanwhile, Islamic clerics and preachers of hate are gladly given visas to train the bombers and jihadists across Europe. Obama could not even shave Nadal Hassan's beard during trial so as not to offend Muslims, despite the fact that the man is a criminal and mass murderer. But I wonder if Americans are not offended when a jihadist Mohammed Yousef Abdulazeez answered the call if ISL to kill Americans to mark the end of the 2015 month of Ramadan by killing four marines and wounded three others by unloading heavy barrage of artillery on gun free military bases in Tennessee. And quoting from Mohammed Yousef Abdulazeez online postings in the contest of '' Who among you has got a name that triggers terror like me? you have the opportunity to act now, forget about your material being and get more rewards in Muslim paradise before the opportunity pass you by." in reference to ISIL call for Muslims to carry out attacks on American and other Western targets and get more reward from Allah during the month of Ramadan. One thing is certain, the murderer gunned down like a rabid dog who he was, has no place in Jehovah's paradise but will join his mentor who brain washed him with the evil teachings of the Quran [Mohammed] in the pit of hellfire where they belong. Yousef, a university qualified engineer was not ignorant or poor but succumbed to a false doctrine, and we now know that the pain he suffered from barrage of bullets that took him down was nothing compared to mosquito sting as Mohammed lied to him, but high threshold bone crushing and belly bursting agonising pain that will hasten his unglorified journey to the bottomless pit of hell.

And if ISIL could invoke the Quran to inspire and claim responsibility for massive and shocking bombings that killed about 130 people and injured about 150 others while celebrating the end of Ramadan 2015 in Iraqi market, where dead Muslim kids were taken away in vegetable cartoons, then it will take a naively imbecilic mind to call Islam a religion of peace that can guarantee any reward in heaven, since all it rewards its followers on earth is death and carnage.

COMMON SENSE SOLUTION TO TERRORISM.

Elimination by Subtraction;- Any Islamic terrorist like Mohammed Yousef Abdulazeez caught or die in the act should have his/her household and relatives stripped of their citizenship, their assets sold by government and the money used to deport them to their beloved homeland of Iraq, Pakistan, Iran, Saudi Arabia or any part of the world they originated from. This will enable them devote their full loyalty to their homeland

and religion, and guess what?, by the time they found themselves in the war ravaged, famine prone and disease infested land of theirs, they will know what good the west has meant and done to them and what a great opportunity of a life time they have lost. They should never be allowed to come back to any western nation to cause terror and this will act as permanent deterrent to other would be Islamic terrorists still lurking in the west and who will not want to go back to live in the caves and dens of Afghanistan, where they will not have access to internet cafes, burger king, ken turkey fried chicken, free health and housing benefits, good road, transport system and portable water. If politicians can take this bold steps, the west will be free or at least reduce the number of this cancers in their midst. Every mosques and Muslims in the west should be monitored as potential terror camp and terrorists. because in as much as every Muslims might not be a terrorist, every terrorists so far has been Muslims.

DEADLY ASYLUM SEEKERS;-

Matthew 5.7 told us "Blessed are the merciful, for they shall obtain mercy. I was shocked to death when I learnt that on the Mediterranean sea while some Muslim asylum seekers trying to run away from ISIL and president Asad's massacres in Syria, Iraq and other parts of Muslim nations towards Italy to run away from home deaths, but on the high seas, their illegal boat ran into turbulence and was sinking. There were a handful of Christian migrants in the boat caught in the same trouble with the Muslims, and the Christians were praying to God through their faith and calling their professed Messiah Jesus Christ to save the boat and as He is known to be good at commanding turbulent storm to be still.

The bunch of hate filled Muslims who are scholars of prophet Mohammed who thought them it is justified to kill Christians and Jews and unbelievers anywhere, anytime, told the Christians to stop praying in the name of Jesus Christ but rather in the name of Allah. When the Christians refused to deny their faith and their Lord Jesus Christ, the miracle worker and the saviour of the world, who has ordered the turbulent sea to "Peace be still" in the days of the apostle, the same peace and still they were only once again asking for themselves and co travellers on the boat. The deadly Muslim asylum seekers did not hesitate to invoke the hate, evil doctrine and barbarism they represents by throwing the Christians one after the other into the open seas to their deaths, and each time shouting their deadly and evil mantra, Allah Akbar.

When you are in the grip of death and looking for a rescuer, the last thing to cross your mind is to persecute another people and plot to kill but to rather concentrate on your own safety, but in Islam, it is an act worship to hate, persecute and to kill, even if there is a drop of blood left in you. So before the west open there borders to the so called asylum seekers from the war ravaged Islamic nations and based on the actions of the terrorists granted asylums in the past, they better open their eyes and brains to the danger of their new tenants from the middle east.

The Expected Islamic Messiah: The Imam Mahdi

The Messiah is one that saves and delivers people from bondage – the ultimate perfect being who bears the likeness of God. To the Christians, the Messiah is Jesus Christ. He promised his followers that he was going to his Father in heaven to prepare a place for them, and he would come and take them to himself so that where he is, they would be there also.

The Jews are still awaiting the arrival of their messiah, even though they do not know what form he will take. The Muslims are expecting their messiah, whom they believe is Imam Mahdi, the perfect human being who will restore justice on earth and rule the caliphate with the law of Allah.

In 2005 the United Nations General Assembly President Ahmadinejad announced his messiah to the entire world, and it seems he could no longer wait for his arrival in prayer. He said, "O mighty Lord, I pray to you to hasten the emergence of your last repository, the promised one, the perfect and pure human being, the one that will fill this world with justice and peace."

It seems that every Dick, Tom, and Harry is expecting a messiah, but who is the real messiah?

From the preceding prayer of Ahmadinejad, we know that his messiah is to emerge from somewhere unknown, but if the story from the Iranian ayatollahs is anything to go by, he will emerge from a well he entered as a youth, reappearing as a fully grown man of wisdom. But no human being has ever died and gone to heaven or hell and returned to this world to rule on earth; it has never happened and never will. So, if the deceased prophet

Mohammed is the one that Muslims are still waiting for, I am sure their wait will last forever. Even those who reappeared from their graves when Jesus Christ rose from the dead quickly disappeared back into the world of the dead.

What credentials of humility, humanity, and justice will Prophet Mohammed bring back to earth if he is somehow given the chance of re-emergence as Imam Mahdi, and where and when would he have gained them? Was it not Mohammed that took pride in using severed heads as trophies and built castles with human skulls? He authorized the beheading of women and children and committed the most egregious war crimes in human history, all in the name of his religion. Even if he had a change of heart and tactics in his grave, he would never come back to the world to carry out those changes. Ironically, all Muslims preach about Imam Mahdi bringing sanity to the world, but they never stop killing and causing insanity. The Ahmadiya brand of Islam is chased and killed like rabid dogs by other Muslims, as they are accused of preaching a messenger different from the prophet Mohammed simply for trying to preach a less harsh and less barbaric form of Islam, and yet the Ahmadiya Jamaat also preach daily about the return of Imam Mahdi. To the hard line Islamists, you are a traitor if you are not " Mohammed" or fire brand Muslim enough.

More confusing still, a messiah is supposed to take adherents to heaven, but the Mahdi's interest is to continue a reign of terror on earth and impose the Sharia law. This can be nothing but another falsehood from the pit of hell and an attempt to mimic the second coming of the true Messiah, Jesus Christ. The Muslims will make an apocalypse happen, using their bomb of Armageddon, and whoever makes this happen will simply install himself as the Mahdi of the caliphate. This is currently being attempted by ISIS. If their commander, Al Baghdadi, is able to wage his war and defeat the world, he will declare himself as the Imam Mahdi. The true Messiah will not emerge from a worldly office or caliphate but, rather, he will take people who diligently worship Jehovah God to heaven.

The only Messiah of humankind is Jesus Christ, so you had better abandon Mahdi and follow Jesus Christ if you want to go to paradise. Jesus Christ is not coming to order your flogging or beheading on earth; he has prepared a place for you in his Father's kingdom so that you can be there with him.

The global turbulence that the Islamists will cause will not be resolved quietly because they always enjoy being in the news. They are attention seekers who want to be perceived as doing the will of their god, no matter how horrible their acts are. It's similar to how they make so much noise about thirty days of Ramadan fasting so that people know they are giving up food and to deceive people into thinking that they are worshiping the true God. Think about it: Who would fast to the true God and still send suicide bombers out to kill worshippers of the same religion and other innocent people, even in their shrines or mosques? But belief it or not, Muslim will forever continue to kill with ignominy as Mohammed has lied to them that the Ramadan fast will always melt away any of their sins, even if it is sin of murder.

The Killing of the Serpent and the Great Pandemonium

The Great Serpent

The serpent is another name for the devil, Satan, Lucifer, and the great deceiver of mankind. He is the treacherous and dangerous being, the evil one.

If you have followed this spirit-inspired book closely up to this page, I am convinced that the Holy Spirit has given you understanding of the danger we face as a human race as well as understanding of the Great Serpent.

Jehovah told us about the character of the serpent in Genesis 3: 1–5.

And the serpent was more subtle than any beast of the field which the Lord God had made. And he said unto the woman, Yea, hath God said, ye shall not eat of every tree of the garden? And the woman said unto the serpent, we may eat of the fruit of the trees of the garden; But of the fruit of the tree which is in the midst of the garden, God hath said, ye shall not eat of it, neither shall ye touch it, lest you die. And the serpent said unto the woman, ye shall not surely die; For God doth know that in the day ye eat thereof, then your eyes shall be opened, and ye shall be as gods, knowing good and evil.

The serpent, in this context, is Lucifer, who communicated with man in the form of a snake. As we all know, natural snakes never speak, but Satan has the power to possess any being or object that is a weakling or that made his or her mind available to him; in the case of Eve, Satan saw her as the weakling among the first two humans. Lucifer also knew the power of a woman to convince a man with her sensual ability. Before Adam and Eve knew what was really happening, they had both eaten the forbidden fruit and sinned.

Lucifer did not waste time in his mission to cause separation and discord between God and his beloved human creations. He said, "Ye shall surely not die for God doth know that in the day you eat thereof, then your eyes shall be opened, and ye shall be as gods" (v. 5). Read the word "gods" as "evil idols" like what Lucifer became following the great battle in heaven that made God cast him out. Lucifer essentially told them, "Join me, folks. Don't mind your God. Become gods like me, and together we shall fight him."

In Genesis 3: 15, Jehovah said, "I will put enmity between thee and the woman, and between thy seed and her seed; it shall bruise thy head and thou shall bruise his heel." The seeds of Satan are evil and strong – the Ishmaelite's, or Muslims.

Jehovah also informed us about the children of the snake in Genesis 16: 11–12. "And the angel of the Lord said unto her, Behold, thou art with a child, and shalt bear a son and shalt call his name Ishmael, because the Lord hath heard your affliction. And he will be a wild man; his hands will be against every man, and every man's hand against him; and he shall dwell in the presence of all his brethren." Just like snake who bruise humans on the heel and humans bruise him on the head.

The Bible says that human children will bruise the seeds of the snake in the head, and the seeds of the snake will bruise the human seeds on the heel. Now that we know the seeds of Lucifer, the serpent, represent Muslims, why are we surprised that Muslims often behead or slit the throats of their victims. These descendants of the snake must have agreed to do this before the descendants of Adam and Eve think of crushing their heads. What a clever move!

No wonder Muslims have no ambition other than to behead the saints. We read in Revelation 20: 4 "And I saw the thrones, and they sat upon them. And judgement was given unto them; and I saw the souls of men that were beheaded for the witness of Jesus, and for the word of God, and which not worshipped the beast, neither his image, neither had received his marks upon their foreheads, or in their hands and they lived and reigned with Christ a thousand years."

In Christian paradise, Jehovah gave crowns to those who were killed in persecution for their witness of Christ and the word of God and those who did not worship the beast.

Who is this beast, and what are the marks he put on the foreheads and hands of those who follow him?

The beast is Lucifer, the snake, the Antichrist and enemy of God and Jesus Christ. The beast's worshippers are the Muslims, and their religion is Islam. As mentioned previously, the marks on their foreheads are the dark patch formed on the foreheads of all Muslims from bumping their foreheads on the ground five times a day when they pray to their idol, Allah. The marks on their hands are the counting beads used when they pray and which they also hold when they pass a beheading or stoning. The leader of Boko Haram in Nigeria was seen on television clutching Islamic prayer beads, and a horrible horn-like dark patch, the sign of the beast, was prominent on his forehead.

The end shall not be well for Lucifer, the great deceiver. The heavens have rejected him, and the earth shall also eject him. He will be destroyed alongside his followers, and then the world will know peace.

Revelation 20: 10 clearly states, "And the devil that deceived them was cast into the lake of fire and brimstone, where the beast and the false prophet are, and shall be tormented day and night for ever and ever." This refers to the pit of hell, the everlasting torment chamber for Lucifer and his false prophet, Mohammed. They will be sent there for deceiving the world and misleading those who could have been followers of Christ and worshippers of Jehovah. Anyone who abandons the jihadi killing machine and follows Jesus Christ shall surely escape the lake of fire.

If the prophet Mohammed teaching his followers to behead non-Muslims and to show no mercy when cutting babies in half while the parents stand by is not an act of deception, then what else can it be? Jehovah God does not want the death of sinners; he wants them to repent and get their sins washed away.

The Killing of the Serpent

Killing the serpent will not be easy; there will be a mighty uproar and upheaval. The beast will fight with all its might and fury, tearing apart everything in its path. It will be a battle between good and evil, between the people choosing the narrow path leading to salvation and those choosing the wide way that leads to destruction.

The first leg of this battle has been fought before, when the followers of the beast battled with all those who did not carry the mark of the beast on their heads and their hands. They killed Jews, Christians, and other people for whom Jesus was anxiously waiting to deliver to himself – idol worshippers and other sinners. The jihadists led by Mohammed beheaded them all until the Western nations, led by the British, pushed back one of the serpent's many heads and stopped the massacre of more innocents and preventing the spread of Islam.

President Thomas Jefferson, one of the US founding fathers, saw first-hand the evil and barbarity of Islam, and he warned the world about it. From 1801 to 1805, the First Barbary War, also known as the Tripolitania War or the Barbary Coast War, was one of two wars fought between the United States of America and the Barbary States in northwest Africa. These states were made up of the Ottoman provinces of Tripoli, Algiers, and Tunis that all enjoyed the independent sultanate of Morocco. The Barbary States made fortunes by hijacking US and European vessels and abducting millions of Americans and Europeans for ransom. They inflicted death, misery, and sorrow on others to make enormous gain. They even sold thousands of the people they abducted as slaves including Britons and Americans.

In those fearsome and deadly days, the Catholic Church formed a humanitarian aid group that raised millions of dollars as ransom to rescue poor people who could not raise the ransom money demanded by their Islamic captors. This gesture rather promoted the ugly entrenchment of Islam and helped finance it, but it was done in the interest of saving souls. Therefore, the Catholic mission had no choice but to join community of God-fearing nations to save humanity from the cancer of Islam at that time.

Thomas Jefferson followed in the footsteps of the Crusaders to wage war on the barbarians. However, Thomas Jefferson eventually refused to pay ransom and discouraged other nations from doing so, to prevent their wealth acquisition from inhumane behaviour. Through Congress, he also authorized the first military conflict by the United States on foreign land and sea, and it ruthlessly crushed the savagery of the Barbary States. Did I hear you say that sounds like following in the footsteps of the jihadi? Mohammed attracted a large followership of rogues and looters who joined Islam just to kill Jews, Christians, and others, selling them as slaves and making a profit from their victims' possessions. It also looks like what the Islamic State is doing today.

President Thomas Jefferson saw the ugly ideology of Islam during a meeting with an Arab ambassador wherein Jefferson questioned the morality of Islamic nations waging war on other nations that caused them no harm. The Islamic ambassador responded, "It is an important teaching of the Koran and the prophet for all Mussulmen to wage war and kill the infidels – that is, non-believers, wherever they are found in any part of the world and that every jihadist killed in such battle shall go to paradise and receive comfort."

But times have changed. An old adage states, "A chick might not have any knowledge of the fury of the killer eagle, but the chick's mother will never play the game of carelessness when dealing with the killer eagle." The founding fathers of America identified the barbarity of Islam, but due to a lack of experience, President Obama did not acknowledge its barbarity.

Obama in his political promise has refused to send boot on the ground in Iraq and Syria to knock out ISIL, but rather covertly supply war equipment's directly to ISIL via Iraqi military who end up abandoning America's finest war machines for easy grab by ISIL to advance their terror mission. I strongly belief in my spirit that this is a clever way of arming Islamic State by President Obama. After all, Obama has being a strong supporter of Islam and not a defender of Israel and Christians.

To defeat ISIL we need a good American leader that is ready to overwhelm every territory gained by ISIL with swarm of soldiers like locust covering a corn field, killing every jihadist local or foreign, capture or kill Al Baghdadi and his followers, recapture or destroy all military hardware they have received from Obama via Iraq and destroy their headquarters and command and control centres. America and his Arab and European allies can achieve this feat within six months, after all, President W.H Bush and allies finished their jobs Iraq and Afghanistan within a tinkle of an eye.

King Abdullah of Jordan saved Christian refugees and gave them refuge in his land but Obama refused to send planes to airlift persecuted Christians in the middle east to safety in America and other western nations, As a Christian, I am yet to see any sign of Christianity in President Obama with global persecution, holocaust and genocide of Christians under his nose and he did nothing. No wonder, Obama said America is no more a Christian nation.

I only hope American Christians will vote with their faith and not their colour after Obama and vote for a candidate and a party that will restore Christianity to its rightful global place.

Unfortunately, it seems the Antichrist is winning the game at the moment. Iran is winning the race to acquire nuclear weapons capability. Together with other twenty-first-century Islamic states, they may be very close to releasing the bomb of Armageddon. Some close officials of Barack Obama have called Prime Minister Benjamin Netanyahu a coward in respect to Iran's nuclear weapons. President Obama referred to Benjamin Netanyahu as an evil he has to deal with every day in a careless moment with the then French president Nicolas Sarkozy caught on microphone. Only Jehovah can help Israel, Jews, and Christianity now, as it seems people in high places – principalities and powers – are close to waging war.

The Great Pandemonium

Our Lord and Saviour, Jesus Christ, has warned us of the chaos and pandemonium the world shall witness in the end-day catastrophe that Islam will cause in an effort to make the world submit to Allah. Their battle strategy will be to kill anyone who is not with them, as we have already begun to witness. The jihadists' battle and the pandemonium they cause shall be of an apocalyptic scale.

Matthew 24: 15–20 warns, "When ye therefore shall see the abomination of desolation, spoken of by Daniel the prophet, stand in the holy place, (whoso reads, let him understand:) Then let them that which be in Judea flee into the mountains: Let him which is on the housetop not come down to take anything out of his house: Neither let him which is in the field return back to take his clothes. And woe unto them that are with child, and to them that give suck in those days! But pray ye that your flight be not in the winter, neither on the Sabbath day."

Does this situation sound familiar? The Yazidi tribe in Iraq was chased to Mountain Sinjar by the newly formed Islamic State. Mothers of infants had no time to finish breastfeeding them, and mothers with four children had no time to look for the two that were in the cornfield before fleeing with the two nearby. People on the mountaintop could not go down to rescue their flocks grazing in the valley, and women in labour were abandoned by their midwives. This is just one case carried out by ISIL, the devastation is felt globally. Thousands of dangerous and bloodthirsty cohesive groups are waiting, and thousands more are in the making, not to mention the millions of lone wolves waiting to bite. The world will be awash with terror if this Armageddon is not nipped in the bud. But the world will not fold their arms while jihadists roam and chop off heads freely. Just like the Crusaders and Thomas Jefferson led battles on land, sea, and air to defeat the Barbary army, a time shall come that anyone who sees a Muslim will be obligated to kill him and save the world. We can hope and pray that the jihadists will renounce their evil ways and repent before the world is sick and tired of their wickedness.

The Second Coming of Jesus Christ, the Messiah

Jesus Christ informed us that he was going to his Father to prepare a place for us. John 14: 1–4 says, "Let not your heart be troubled; ye believe in God, believe also in me. In my Father's house are many mansions: if it were not so, I would have told you. I go to prepare a place for you. And if I go and prepare a place for you, I will come again and receive you unto myself; that where I am, there you may be also. And whither I go ye know, and the way you know."

This statement starts with a reassuring and comforting line: "Let not your heart be troubled" (v. 1). He knew that his followers would face many heart-breaking moments of persecution in this world and will be greatly troubled by the Antichrists of the world. The world would hate them so much so that they would be longing for an escape route from their aggressors; therefore, he made a grand plan to move them to safety in his Father's house.

Have you ever wondered what would make Jesus Christ want to come back to this world after the unmerited cruelty it meted out to him? He cannot stand idly by and do nothing when the collective fury of Lucifer and his jihadist hirelings behead every living soul that refuses to bow to the beast or receive his marks upon them.

When the grounds are cleared for the Islamic-induced arrival of Imam Mardi – with all the sorrow and agony of unimaginable apocalyptic dimensions – and the physical reign of Lucifer on earth about to commence,

Jesus Christ shall come with his band of angelic armies and take his beloved home to his Father's mansion.

But no human can predict the apocalypse, the time of the second coming, or the end of the world. Not even the angels in heaven knows. But in Matthew 24: 21–22, Jesus Christ warns, "For then shall be great tribulation, such as was not since the beginning of the world to this time, no, nor ever shall be. And except those days should be shortened, there should no flesh be saved: but for the elect's sake those days shall be shortened."

Jesus Christ was right then and forever shall be. Tribulations such as deliberately flying jets into public buildings with human beings as the primary target, bombing commuters on buses and subways, suicide bombings in busy supermarkets, and beheadings of innocent journalists and humanitarian workers or colleagues because they refused to bow down to the beast of Islam. These and other acts of unbelievable terror have not been seen before on the earth.

Lord, you shortened and nipped in the bud atrocities of the jihadists in the past by sending the Crusaders and Thomas Jefferson. I trust you that even today, with principalities and powers and people in high places waging Lucifer's war against Christ and his followers, you will send your holy warriors from heaven to team up with your soldiers on earth and prevent this bomb of Armageddon so that the elect shall be saved. Amen.

Printed in the United States
By Bookmasters